# LEADING GROWTH

# LEADING GROWTH

THE PROVEN FORMULA
FOR CONSISTENTLY
INCREASING REVENUE

ANTHONY IANNARINO

WILEY

Published by John Wiley & Sons, Inc., Hoboken, New Jersey.
Published simultaneously in Canada.

For general information on our other products and services or for technical support, please contact our Customer Care Department within the United States at (800) 762-2974, outside the United States at (317) 572-3993 or fax (317) 572-4002.

Wiley also publishes its books in a variety of electronic formats. Some content that appears in print may not be available in electronic formats. For more information about Wiley products, visit our web site at www.wiley.com.

*Library of Congress Cataloging-in-Publication Data is Available:*

ISBN: 9781119890331 (cloth)
ISBN: 9781119890348 (ePub)
ISBN: 9781119890355 (ePDF)

Cover design: Paul McCarthy

SKY10035534_072922

# Contents

# Prologue

My friend Tom Strasburg had a high school buddy named Jeff. Jeff wasn't exactly certain what to do after high school, so he joined the army. Jeff's experience in boot camp was the stereotypical representation you've seen in every war movie.

Jeff's drill sergeant worked his recruits hard, relentlessly telling them they were the worst recruits he'd ever seen in his many years training soldiers. He insisted they were not fit for his beloved army. Over several weeks, the recruits got used to the insults until the comments were expected, regardless of their performance. Then one day, the drill sergeant changed from insults to a challenge.

In the evening, as he had his soldiers in formation, dog-tired and hungry, he'd challenge someone to step forward to fight him. He'd badger them, belittle them, curse at them, insult them, doing everything in his power to compel someone to engage him in combat. The drill sergeant was tough as steel, and he could also make their lives miserable. As you might imagine, no one stepped up. There was little upside for accepting his challenge, and an enormous downside.

One day, after the drill sergeant had spent weeks prodding the soldiers to muster up the courage to fight him, he said, "Isn't there a single one of you with the courage to step up and tangle with me?" Having heard this same challenge for weeks, Jeff took one step forward without turning his head toward the drill sergeant. No one said a word for what seemed an eternity.

The drill sergeant looked at Jeff, pointed directly at him, turned to the other soldiers, and said, "There is your squad leader." Without another word, the drill sergeant turned and walked off the field.

# Foreword

THE KEYSTONE, AN architectural concept related to the building of an arch, is the stone in the middle that bears the entire weight of the structure. Without the keystone, the arch would collapse.

Over a 20-year career leading sales organizations of various sizes, I have come to recognize the frontline sales leader as the sales organization's "keystone." Any program, initiative, even the very sales culture itself, will succeed based on the strength of the sales leadership team. With an ineffective frontline sales leadership team, however, the sales structure is at risk of collapse.

This belief does not minimize the importance of our individual sellers who are putting forth an untold amount of energy and effort each day to support prospects and customers to improve their results. Rather, **elite sellers demand elite leaders**. Elite leaders are talent magnets who attract, develop, coach, and retain the great sellers who are the difference-makers of an organization.

While the role of a sales leader can be called the most critical function in a sales organization, it is also among the most difficult to master. The primary reason for this is that an effective sales leader requires mastery of both selling *and* sales leadership.

Sales and sales leadership are in the same family, yet the roles and skills required to do them well are quite different.

If a sales leader understands leadership without understanding how their salespeople must operate, they will have challenges improving their seller's effectiveness. This will ultimately cost the leader followership and, eventually, their role.

Conversely, if the leader is a sales expert with limited or no knowledge of leadership, they will be nothing more than a glorified salesperson (to quote my friend, Mike Weinberg, "a hero not a hero maker") with a lid to their impact that ultimately lands them back in a sales role.

The importance of the function on the success of an organization, combined with the challenges the role presents, makes it all the more curious how little training and ongoing development sales leaders receive in many organizations. The training of a sales leader is often fractional compared to supervisory functions in other areas of a business, and there are many organizations who still do minimal training of their sales leaders.

The driver of this, from my perspective, is a generation of senior sales leaders who were also not trained to lead and carry with them the belief that "I didn't get trained and I figured it out, so they can too." This logic affects attrition rates for the role itself, while also impacting the lives of an untold number of sellers who have the misfortune of placing their careers in the hands of an incompetent leader.

I am fortunate to have worked with great people and had success with great teams, though in my first leadership assignment I chose the path of most resistance. I knew little about what I was doing beyond that we were going to move fast and sell a lot. I made every mistake there was to make as a new leader and while (luckily) delivering over quota results, I was winning in spite of myself rather than because of myself.

The turning point in my leadership career was the moment I realized that as a sales leader, I controlled two things and two things alone. The more I focused on exerting control in these two areas at the expense of all others, the more effective I became. The first was who was on my team, and the second, how well I had equipped those people to succeed.

I reached this conclusion while reflecting on my frustration with people on my team who were underperforming. I have always operated with the belief that anything that happens to me is my fault and my responsibility. I determined that if someone on my team was underperforming, it was a byproduct of my decisions, in one of two ways.

If a salesperson was underperforming, it was either because I sent them out into the field unprepared to perform in the role, which was my decision not to adequately prepare them, or because I decided to keep that person in that role after they had proven over a measurable period that they were unable or unwilling to do the things required to perform in the role.

As a leader, if I recruited and selected the best people, I would have the best team. If I relentlessly worked to train and develop my great people, I would have the best team. If I had the highest of standards and enforced those standards, I would have the best team. (Note that the lowest behavior a leader is willing to tolerate is the actual standard, not what is spoken or printed on the wall.)

These were lessons with immense value, and ones through which my life and many other lives could have been improved had I learned them sooner.

It is the importance of the role, the challenge of the role, the lack of training, and the pivotal leadership lessons learned along the way that frame the significance of the book you are holding, *Leading Growth*.

I have been a long-time reader of Anthony's work. His daily blog is required reading for all sales and sales leadership professionals. What has always drawn me to Anthony is that while most sales content is a tactical explanation or "do this," his cerebral style challenges the reader to think about what they are doing and why they are doing it, and ensures appropriate preparation to maximize value in every interaction.

What he has done with *Leading Growth* is create the ultimate unification of both the art and the science of Sales Leadership. The book embraces the requirements of elite leadership, while not ignoring the reality that there are principles of management that must be upheld in the day-to-day actions of the role.

What makes *Leading Growth* such a valuable book is that it covers the critical but traditional elements of sales leadership like accountability, training and coaching effectiveness, opportunity reviews, and selecting talent.

Where this book is different and takes the reader to a new level is a dive into the intangible aspects of the role. He takes us through a framework for crafting a vision and communicating it in a way that resonates and wins hearts and minds, and explores how to set standards and nonnegotiables. The reader is taught to distinguish between commitment and compliance along leadership styles and their situational applicability. Even something as critical (but rarely considered) as protecting your team from non-sales work is addressed in *Leading Growth*.

These lessons are what make this book so impactful. They are the lessons all leaders need to know but are so often overlooked unless learned the hard way.

For new leaders, even those in companies who provide great leadership training, this book establishes a strong foundation to succeed early and sustainably. For a new leader thrown to the proverbial wolves, the experiential recollection of the things elite leaders do has incalculable value.

For an experienced sales leader, you will learn both new techniques and philosophies to add to your repertoire, while being reminded of things you did when you started out but have since taken for granted over time. It will challenge you to master or remaster the fundamentals of the role.

For executives, this book provides a blueprint of skills and expectations to build or elevate an elite frontline leader function, which has immeasurable benefits for any organization.

Leadership carries with it a significant responsibility. When people come to work for us they are making the tacit statement that of all the career options that are available to them, the best decision for their career and their future is to put it in our hands.

As leaders we must be the bridge, through coaching, development, and accountability, from where our people are today to wherever they want to go in the future. If our people believe we represent that bridge, they will stay and grow with us. If we shirk our responsibility, our people will go elsewhere to find a leader they believe can get them where they want to go.

As a salesperson or a leader, the best career advice I can offer is to find leaders and find companies who are fanatical about developing people. Your productivity, income, career advancement, and quality of life will thank you for it.

My hope is that readers of this book will come away with the knowledge and foundation to flourish today while being inspired to build a better future. It allows readers to raise their standard of excellence for themselves as well as their leaders.

The future of the sales profession will be positively altered as the development of sales leadership gains prominence. Leaders who are well-developed will embrace the responsibility of developing future leaders, who in turn master developing our salespeople. The tide of the profession will rise permanently as a result.

—Mike Jeffrey
Vice President of HCM Solutions Sales, Paychex

# Introduction

THE SHORT, TRUE story that makes up the prologue is one of the best definitions of leadership you might ever encounter. It provides the idea that a person can step up and take accountability for what promises to be a difficult outcome, and in doing so, become a leader. The drill sergeant had no intention of fighting any of the soldiers in his charge. Instead, he wanted to see who would step up, who would do what was necessary when pressed to do something difficult and unpleasant.

I have no military experience myself, so beyond the prologue and the following story from *Ender's Game*, by Orson Scott Card, you will find only sales leadership, because it is something I have practiced and studied long enough to write this book.

*Ender's Game* is a science fiction book about a military force that identifies very young geniuses, taking them to space to prepare to fight aliens that almost destroyed their planet. Author Orson Scott Card begins his introduction by sharing how he came up with the main idea in the book. When he read the three-volume book *The Army of the Potomac* by Bruce Catton, what struck Card was the fact that three different generals led

1

the Union Army, all of them failing for one reason or another. General Ulysses S. Grant, the fourth leader, took over with the same army, the same enemy, the same leaders, the same horses, and same terrain as the generals he replaced. The difference between Grant and the others was his willingness to use the army as an extension of his will.

One of the things you notice about leaders who struggle is that they don't treat their sales force as an extension of their will. A large part of this book is going to provide you with the strategies and structures that will make your sales force an extension of your will. You cannot reach your revenue growth goals; instead, your team must meet their goals for you to meet yours. Growth isn't something that happens due to good luck, working for a great company, incredible products or services, weak competitors, or any other external factors one might credit for an increase in revenue.

Growth only comes from strong and effective leadership and a team focused on revenue growth.

## The Revenue Growth Formula

The formula for revenue growth is simple and straightforward. You start with your expected revenue going into a period and subtract the churn you expect before adding in the net new revenue you expect to acquire.

Existing Revenue – Churn + Net New Revenue
$$= \$15,000,000 - \$2,000,000 + 5,000,000 = \$18,000,000$$

The existing revenue is what you are certain to capture from your existing clients and their commitments, contracts, and orders. Because these deals were done in the past, there is little you can do about the revenue you start with going into a year or a quarter. Every business experiences churn, and some part of that churn is beyond your control. The fewer clients you lose, the easier it is to grow your revenue. That leaves us with net new revenue, the area where what you do can create revenue or cause you to stagnate. In the worst case, not creating enough net new revenue can cause you to experience what some describe as "negative growth," a euphemism for "shrinking."

The revenue growth formula is simple, but it isn't easy. There are three ways you can grow revenue:

1. Sell more to your existing clients.
2. Acquire new clients.
3. Raise your prices.

As a sales leader or a sales manager, you are responsible for the first two. You may also be charged with raising prices, but that decision may come from your executive leadership. However, if pricing is within your control, raising prices can contribute to revenue growth. Ideally, you pursue all three strategies simultaneously, especially if you have aggressive sales targets.

With a simple formula and only three levers needed, why is revenue growth difficult for sales organizations, sales leaders, sales managers, and their teams? If you've ever had the feeling that professional B2B sales is increasingly more difficult, you aren't alone. There are powerful forces at work that make revenue growth more challenging than ever. Some of these forces are external, making it something outside of a sales organization's direct control. These forces are going to require you and your team to adapt and evolve. There are also internal changes that plague sales organizations and make revenue growth difficult—or impossible.

Sales organizations unaware of these challenges will struggle to understand why revenue growth eludes them. For now, don't worry about the challenges to growth, because all of them can be addressed by good and effective sales leadership. Let's start by understanding what these challenges are so you can identify them, communicate them to your team, address them effectively, and grow your revenue.

## External Challenges to Revenue Growth

The massive, disruptive, and evolutionary change in B2B sales is the result of changes in the environment that have made it harder for buyers and decision-makers to effect change in their company, as well as successfully completing their buyer's journey, with over 54 percent ending in a decision to do nothing.

The story here isn't about how sales has changed, but how buying has become more difficult for your prospective clients. Let's look at six major factors that can contribute to an inability to create revenue growth, starting with one of the greatest forces on the planet.

### The Internet and Information Disparity

The internet has removed a lot of what a salesperson might have shared with the client, making much of it unnecessary. Your prospective clients can find information about your company, your products and services, and your clients on your website. In fact, if you have a functioning website, they can probably get deeper into their buyer's journey than you might imagine. Salespeople who don't create any greater value for a client than reciting facts about their company provide no value greater than a Google search or a query on DuckDuckGo.

While some "experts" suggest the client now has information parity, the truth is that the information parity is rather limited and is mostly facts about your company. The information disparity that allows the salesperson to be valuable isn't something that is easily captured on a website.

What is missing is your sales force's experience, the subtle insights gleaned through their experience over many years helping clients, and the ability to help create a paradigm shift that would cause the client to change. The paradigm shift is accomplished when a salesperson teaches the client something about themselves and replaces their outdated assumptions with a higher-resolution lens through which to view decisions about their future.

Although it is true your team has insights the client could never acquire on a website, the truth is that your clients now spend a large amount of their time pursuing better results by conducting research without the help of a salesperson.

## Uncertainty and the Status Quo

Our current environment is one of constant, accelerating, disruptive change, dislocating decision-makers who feel the unrelenting speed as uncertainty. The more difficult it is to predict anything about the future other than "what's next," the more challenging it is to make decisions about the future. When you're uncertain about the future, it feels safer to avoid change, as you might make things worse. When this is true, contacts who don't want to make a bad decision often wait until they have greater certainty. Many of those who wait will find this same environment forcing them to change on a timeline not of their choosing.

The problem for the sales force is that the uncertainty created by the increasingly complex world isn't likely to change any time soon—if it ever does. If you ever wondered why the sales conversation your team has with their prospects comes in fits and starts, making progress only to go dark, it's because the prospect has learned to live with the devil they know. The reason the promising deals in your pipeline stall or die prematurely is because of the client's uncertainty.

## The Unforgiving Reality of the Consensus Sale

I remember the first time I walked into a client's conference room to be greeted by fourteen people sitting around a giant table. The senior leader introduced the team as "the task force." In the past, your sales force might have called on "the decision-maker," the person with the "authority" to sign a contract and agree to pricing. Because leaders want their team to have the autonomy to buy what they need, choosing the partner they believe to be the best fit and accountable for results, leaders allow them to build consensus among their team—or increasingly, several teams.

This difficult, political, and messy process often ends in a no-decision, as some teams believe that consensus means a unanimous decision instead of a simple plurality. It is almost certain that your team has never been trained or taught to how to manage a sales conversation with many decision-makers, decision-shapers, and stakeholders. Even with a framework, it's difficult at best, impossible at worst. Your sales force is working to build consensus with a group of people who may be at odds over the decision to change, how to change, or what the right decision might be. But even more, having more people in the conversation has changed the sales process.

## The Nonlinearity of the Sales Conversation

For thirty-four years, sales organizations have used a linear sales process to sell "solutions." In truth, the sales process was not designed to help the client as much as ensuring every salesperson followed the same steps, checking off the outcomes under each stage of their process before "closing the gate" and moving into the next stage. In early 2010, I wrote a blog post confessing that I was "sales process agnostic." My experience convinced me that deals often end up in a location where "turn-by-turn directions are unavailable."

Many buyers now reject the standard solution sales process, finding it lacking. One thing that is clear is that buyers and decision-makers are not concerned about following the well-worn path of yesteryear, mostly because they find it difficult to manage their internal challenges, including consensus. A salesperson can meet with two decision-makers twice and show up to a third meeting to find three fresh, new faces with questions the salesperson had already answered. The fourth meeting may find them with a decision-maker missing. The nonlinearity makes it difficult to control the process and facilitate their buyer's journey. Which leads us to the fact that there is not a single buyer's journey. Instead, there are journeys.

## The Time-Based Nature of Sales Results

Time is too precious to waste. But waste is what you get when you pursue a prospective client, only to have them stall or disengage completely. The factors above cause all kinds of problems when it comes to revenue growth, starting with the fact that a deal that looks certain to cross the line doesn't move for weeks or months.

Missed quarters early in the year can make it more difficult to reach your goals even when you do everything in your power to close the gap. While I am not providing you or your team with an excuse, it is important for you to know that time is a factor that can cause problems growing your revenue. Later, when we explore the primacy of creating new opportunities, you will understand why.

## Competition and Its Impact on Results

One aggressive competitor invaded my city, opening a couple of locations and winning large clients from established players.

To grab a foothold in the market, they employed a "predatory pricing" strategy. At the time, my industry was relatively new and enjoyed rich margins. Business was good for everyone. It was stunning to see the impact one competitor could make in a few months. As the new competitor took over major clients, the margins started coming down faster than I thought possible, as companies that couldn't afford to lose their major accounts lowered their price to retain them.

We don't often recognize the impact of competition as it pertains to growth, whether it is through low pricing, some new advantage, or a sales force effective enough to displace their competition or win the most attractive clients in a territory. You might also have "alternatives" from new models you are now competing against. In any case, competition can make it difficult to grow revenue. The best approach to competition is to be more effective at the sales conversation and create greater value for your prospective clients.

## Internal Challenges to Revenue Growth

The ugly list of external challenges is matched by this equally horrendous list of internal challenges. The upside of these monstrosities is that you can directly work to correct them. That said, they are not pleasant, and all of them impact revenue growth.

### Starting from Behind: The High Cost of Churning Clients

The growth formula suggests that growth comes from net new revenue greater than your churn. I am more than familiar with this challenge, having lost my largest client in the first month of a year, creating a deficit just over $9,000,000. After replacing that revenue to stay even, I lost my second largest client the following January. It was no easier to replace over $8,000,000 the next year. The reason companies create "customer success" roles is because churn is a drag on growth.

You make incremental net new revenue much easier to achieve when you don't have to replace a large amount of lost revenue. You don't want your first net new dollar to be captured after replacing $9,000,000. Addressing this challenge requires all areas of the company to contribute to reducing churn. You may have to show the impact on growth to your executive leaders to get their attention on the high cost of churn.

## Prospecting Problems: Too Little Opportunity Creation

After churn, nothing is more destructive to revenue growth than a sales force that doesn't prospect. When we boil selling down to its essence, it is made up of two outcomes: (1) creating new opportunities, and (2) pursuing and winning those opportunities. Because you cannot close any opportunity without first opening it, "opening is the new closing."

From a lack of accountability to salespeople who don't like to make cold calls, or senior salespeople who believe prospecting is somehow beneath them, we've seen sales leaders improve their results simply by insisting their team prospects and creates the net new opportunities to achieve revenue growth. *Leading Growth* will provide you with a blueprint you can use to increase the number of opportunities your team creates. We'll also address winning more of your opportunities.

## Variability of Performance

It's difficult for civilians (non-salespeople) to understand why some salespeople make selling look easy and others struggle. When two salespeople work for the same company, sell the same solution, compete against the same competitors, share the same pricing, and work for the same sales leader, it can be hard to understand why one succeeds and the other barely gets by.

There is a variability in the performance of different salespeople. Regardless of opinions to the contrary, some salespeople are born with gifts that allow them to make selling look easy. Others become successful salespeople over time. Occasionally, even the gifted experience an unexplainable slump, and the less talented have a streak of won deals. Much of what follows here will help you even out the variability through accountability, communication, and development.

## Effectiveness Problems: Low Win Rates

Up until this book, my primary concern in the prior four have been around increasing the sales force's effectiveness. There is no contribution to revenue from lost deals, and no one wins every deal. But most of the reason salespeople lose deals is because they're not effective at the sales conversation, the only vehicle available for creating a preference to buy from them.

Much of a sales force's effectiveness problems are the result of the legacy approach to sales that no longer works for buyers.

There is another growth formula that sits directly under the revenue growth formula. That formula suggests that the growth of the sales force's effectiveness precedes revenue growth. One way to think of this is that if your team could deliver your revenue growth, they already would have done so. The better your team's performance the greater your growth.

## Losing Time: Too Many Distractions

I have witnessed a phenomenon in businesses large and small. In part, certain salespeople are "mother hens," winning a new client and sitting on it like it's an egg. In some cases, the salesperson works for the client, and people soon believe that person is on the client's team. They generate client reports and deliver them, track down shipments, and retype incorrect invoices.

Anything to keep their giant egg warm and safe. Soon after, they give up prospecting and live on their one account.

The second way a salesperson gets pulled out of sales is when their company asks them to do non-sales-related work. Because the salesperson has the relationship with the client, they are asked to collect past-due payments that should be collected by their accounts receivable department. When operations needs help, they call on the best and most competent person to deal with the client's problem. I dare you to go to your company's operations team and tell them your team has fallen behind on booking new meetings and ask them to volunteer some folks from their team to make cold calls (if you do this, please have someone get a picture of the person's face). There is already too little time for selling. You must protect your team's time.

The combination of the difficult selling environment and the internal challenges of revenue growth require that you lead your sales force consistently and effectively, helping them change their beliefs and their behaviors when and where necessary. The rest of the book is designed to give you the mindset, skill set, and tools necessary to create revenue growth.

## How to Use This Book

This book is written in the order that makes the most sense of the content. Each chapter builds on the preceding chapters, creating a cohesive approach to leading revenue growth. But there is nothing stopping you from identifying the chapter that you believe will help you improve some result you need to improve with some sense of urgency. You may find you need to prioritize two or three chapters before going back and reading the book in the order it appears.

*Leading Growth* is made up of three parts. Each of these parts provides the foundation for what follows. Together it is a cohesive approach to revenue growth. Part I, "Foundations for Growth," helps you set the groundwork for the actions you need to take. These fundamentals—including vision, transformation, and communication—will direct everything you do. Part II, "Taking the Lead," covers the key components of leadership: style, decision-making, and strategy. These influence everything you need to do to grow. Part III, "Accountability, People, and Effectiveness," deals with accountability, including how to cultivate it, what structures you should use to support it, and how to ensure the people on your team are working effectively. It also covers how to increase your team's effectiveness and how to create reliable and accurate forecasts, which underpin accountability efforts. Finally, Part IV, "An Eye to the Future," helps you set your sights on where you're headed. It includes concrete and practical techniques you can use to protect your sales force and tailor the cadence of your activities so your team can maximize their potential.

Leading growth is an ongoing effort, and it relies on finding your rhythm and staying consistent. By the time you reach the last chapter, "Your Next Vision," you'll return to the fundamentals so you and your team can continue to improve and grow.

# PART

# I

# Foundations for Growth

BEFORE YOU UNDERTAKE any growth initiative, you need to set a strong foundation to build on. This foundation has three main components: vision, transformation, and communication. Vision is like the blueprint; it shows you where you're going and acts as a tool you can return to so your growth initiative is coherent, clear, and consistent. Transformation is what you need to do to support the growth you're targeting. It's the action behind the vision. Communication is how you share your vision with your team and enroll them in your transformation.

# 1

## Vision

LEADING GROWTH AND increasing your revenue begins with a vision of your future results. The reason to find your vision first is that it's the foundation of everything that follows. You may not have a map to the future you see in your mind's eye, and you might not fully understand how you'll build it, but all of that will come into focus as you build your vision. Without a vision, you're simply unlikely to achieve your targeted revenue growth. That's because a vision isn't just an idea: it's a destination, a reason to transform, and a new standard for your sales force. If you cannot see the future you're moving toward, it will be invisible to your team.

A revenue goal should be part of your vision, but not the whole thing. When your vision is compelling enough, you create an opportunity for your team to enroll in an adventure where they can make a difference, grow and develop, and be a part of something important. Enrollment is more powerful than compliance precisely because it requires commitment. Compliance is doing something because you must, not because you want to. When you win your team's hearts and minds, they do more than just clock in and go through the motions. They are working alongside you to make your vision a reality.

Much of this book reveals the mechanics of revenue growth, providing a how-to approach for growing your sales. This chapter will help you develop your vision, a vision that belongs to you alone at first, but one you'll later share with your team.

## What Do You Want?

You must choose what you want from a seemingly infinite number of possibilities, a process that most people find either very easy or nearly impossible. If you need to, you can always refer to an earlier vision and adjust it, so it is right for you and your team and your goals. In a later chapter, we'll look at how to align your sales vision with your company's broader goals. Some leaders know what they want with no prompting, making it very natural for them to see their vision. Others struggle to decide even the broad strokes. Let me share my vision as a sales leader, which I've developed over years, as an example.

- We secure revenue growth from large clients that consider our products and services to be strategically important.
- We create greater value than any competitor, never needing to answer "why us" because our sales conversations have proven we are the right choice.
- We are insight-based and consultative, helping clients with a paradigm shift that causes them to recognize the need to change.
- We spend time each day prospecting, scheduling meetings, and creating new opportunities.
- We have a positive culture of accountability where every member of the team does their part.
- We control the process, facilitating the client's buyer's journey, and we ensure they succeed by helping them make the best decision for their company.
- We command a price higher than our competition because we provide outcomes worth investing more to obtain.
- We continually develop, grow, and help our clients, building our individual client portfolios and making a difference.
- We are the most effective sales force in our industry.

For your own list, it's best to start with your revenue growth goal. In fact, every bullet point on my list targets revenue growth in some way! Oh, and don't worry about getting your vision exactly right on the first attempt. It will change as you pursue it, and it will also become clearer as you move forward.

## Why Do You Want It?

Ecological philosopher Edward Abbey once declared, "Growth for the sake of growth is the ideology of the cancer cell."

Identifying your vision is easier when you understand the reason you want it. My best advice is not to make money the primary motivation for your vision, because that will leave too many people behind. Likewise, avoid something lame like "creating value for our shareholders," as only the board of directors believes that making rich people richer is anyone's primary motivator. It's doubtful that your sales force can tell you the names of three board members or any of your company's institutional investors. A better reason for your vision is something like "reaching our full potential," or "making a greater contribution to our clients' results," or "being the most effective sales force in our company or industry."

Again, here's some more of my vision as an example.

- We pursue large clients because we can make the greatest difference for them by improving their overall results. We also help smaller clients when it makes sense to do so.
- We create more value in the sales conversation because our approach and our experience improve our clients' ability to make decisions that improve their results.
- Because we have greater experience, our insights help our clients avoid mistakes that might harm their business. By providing them with a better view of their business, we lead them toward the better results they need.
- We prospect each day because there are still clients who need our help that we have not yet acquired.
- We facilitate the buyer's journey to prevent each buyer from failing to complete that journey. Our advice and recommendations help them with the conversations they need and allow us to resolve their concerns.
- Because we prioritize sales effectiveness, we are always training and developing the skills and traits central to our craft.
- The evidence of our effectiveness is found in the results we provide our clients and in our revenue growth.
- We enjoy the work we do, and we know that our work makes a difference.

## Identifying Your Full Potential

This may be the first time you have seen what a vision for your team might look like. Take heart: there is little chance your sales team has ever been confronted with a vision like the one you will create and share with them.

A good way to start building your vision is to identify what you believe is your team's full potential. Imagine if every person on your team reached their full potential. Without knowing you or your sales force, I am certain that even your best performers still have untapped potential. Some of your lagging sales reps can certainly improve with the right guidance. In fact, I have seen benchwarmers leave a company and become all-stars under a different manager in a new company.

At first, not everyone on your team will see your vision. A few will recognize that you are pursuing change but insist that your vision is another flavor-of-the-month initiative, one you'll forget about within a few weeks. These people will patiently wait for you to give up. Others will have trouble committing because they aren't certain they will be able to do what will be required of them. And of course, there will be some who see your vision and get excited by the prospect of doing something bigger and more interesting than "going to work."

Don't worry about any of them, because the first section of this book is going to equip you with everything you need to succeed in bringing your vision to life. But first we need to set you up for success.

## Identify the Changes Needed to Create Your Vision

To get your vision built, you need to identify the changes you need to make and the changes you need from your team. Here is a thought experiment to get you started: imagine you are starting with a brand-new team, one scheduled to start work in a week or two. They don't know what to expect, never having worked for you. What would you expect of this new group that you don't expect from your current team? What would you insist they do that would bring your vision to life and ensure you grow your revenue?

A senior sales leader once shared with me that he intended to replace his entire sales force and start over. Beyond the obvious challenge of releasing the entire sales force and hiring all new salespeople, my experience told me his results wouldn't improve. Still, before I could bite my tongue, the words flew out of my mouth: "What are you going to do with the third group?" The senior leader responded, "What do you mean? Say it so I can understand what you're saying!" I explained, "When you hire the second group and have the same set of problems you have now, what are you going to do when you fire them and have to hire a third sales force?" He was not amused, but he understood I was indicting him and his sales managers, who were not engaged with their teams.

The prospect of a fresh start is attractive, but this story shows why you must start where you are with what (and who) you have. It doesn't mean that everyone on your team will want to help you build your vision. Nor does it mean keeping people who aren't interested in growth, development, or even revenue growth. Some may resent having to change, especially if they've only ever known the low standard they've been allowed to maintain. Over time, it may become important for you to add people willing to help you bring your vision to life.

No matter where you start, I can tell you the two greatest threats to your vision and revenue growth: (1) too few opportunities (an activity *and* effectiveness problem) and (2) too few won deals (an effectiveness problem). Fortunately, you will find answers to both problems throughout this book, along with many more strategies to help you reach your growth goals.

## Creating Constructive Tension and Positive Friction

Your vision requires change, a function of constructive tension and positive friction. Without some tension between your current state and your future state, you cannot achieve your vision. Much of that tension arises from the behavioral changes you're asking your team to make. In fact, if there is no tension, it likely means your team isn't taking new actions, a decision that presents a threat to your vision and revenue growth. You can think of tension like a trampoline. When someone pushes against the trampoline, the metal coils securing the fabric push back, launching them skyward. For example, you are certain to have friction around prospecting when you are forced to confront the salespeople on your team who try to avoid cold outreach. You will have others who are not interested in changing the way they sell, or the new standards you require.

Friction shows up in conversations when people reject or oppose your vision. They often argue they shouldn't have to change, but you refuse to relent on the changes that result in revenue growth. In any change initiative, you can count on resistance. This is a positive form of friction, as it prompts a conversation about your future results. Even if a salesperson or two push for an exemption, you must defend your changes, no matter what they are and no matter who is causing the friction. Much of the time, you will create the friction yourself when you require someone to honor your now-higher standards. In fact, I would bet against any initiative succeeding if everyone went along without a word.

It's difficult to ask someone to believe that what they've always done is no longer sufficient, especially when they believe it was the source of their success. Much like a client who's missed an inflection point in their industry, it can be difficult for your sales team to believe that what has always been "good enough" is no longer sufficient. But if what you did in the past really worked to grow your revenue, you wouldn't need a new vision now. You cannot protect your team from the constructive tension and friction that comes from raising your standards, expecting more from every individual, and pursuing your full potential. Without this tension between your new expectations and what was your status quo, you risk losing your vision.

The friction you need to create acknowledges that "what got you here will not get you there." Think of it this way: what you have done until this point was critical to starting this journey to your better future state and the better results that make up your vision. You and your team are well prepared to tackle the changes your vision demands, and if for some reason you are not, keep reading and you'll find what you need here.

Constructive tension and positive friction allow you to move forward. The conversations, the conflict, the questions, and the resistance propel you toward your vision if you continue to communicate and lead your team to collectively pursue your vision.

## Explain Who Your Team Will Become

Both identity and belonging are hardwired in our psychology: we want to know who we are and where we fit. Explaining who your team will become can help people recognize that once they enroll, they will acquire a new identity and belong to something greater than what they were before.

The forces of identity and belonging pull people toward enrollment. That pull doesn't exist if all you want is to make more money or hit a certain sales target. Being part of your team must be something special. Your vision should set your team apart, not just because they're pursuing different goals but because other teams do little more than run out the clock. There are too many people in jobs where there is no vision to guide them or cause them to do their best work. You've probably worked for those companies and in those departments! Your vision needs to protect your team from that fate.

As a leader, how much more engagement would you get if your vision inspired people to give you their best performance, after you've given them your best? How much would your engagement grow? Would you enroll in a vision that makes you part of an elite team working on increasing their effectiveness, making a greater impact on their client's results, and securing results and revenue that exceed anything they've done before?

Identity cuts off the possibility of being something else, while also prescribing new beliefs and new actions. Your vision does not simply apply your team's identity to a new project, but promises to transform them.

## Addressing Threats to Your Vision

The first and largest threat to your vision is the tendency to start with a bang but settle for a fizzle. Specifically, as you move closer to your vision and revenue growth, you may want to lessen the tension and remove the friction. Even when you produce better results, the tension is still necessary. When you let up, you make it easy for your teams to regress and postpone your vision far into the future.

We often overestimate what we can do in a day, a week, a month, or a quarter. But we underestimate what we can accomplish in a year, and we wildly underestimate what we can do in three years. You want to make changes you can sustain for years, knowing that your new disciplines will allow you and your team to realize your vision and maintain revenue growth for as long as you lead them.

There are always obstacles and challenges that threaten your vision, and you must be vigilant in tracking and removing anything that might endanger it. This includes the beliefs and behaviors that work against revenue growth. If your results don't change, your team is not maintaining the appropriate construc-tive tension—instead, they (and you) are tacitly agreeing to a standard too low to deliver your vision.

To start this transformation and build a team that can reach your revenue growth goals, let's look at a set of positive strategies to gain their enrollment.

## *Thirteen Enrollment Strategies*

Several years back, I contacted Seth Godin to ask him about enrollment and how it differs from compliance. Seth was kind enough write a blog post to address this powerful idea, which in turn inspired me to draft a list of ten enrollment strategies. Seth suggested three additional strategies, forming the list you see here.

- **Understand and speak to the seeker's dream.** Everyone wants something. To enroll the members in your team, you need to know what they want. A good leader knows their people well enough to recognize what they want and to speak to their dreams. When you speak to a seeker's dream, you make it easier to enroll them in your vision, as it provides them a way to pursue that dream.
- **Help provide directions to a better future.** When you offer someone a chance to build a better future, enrolling them means providing them with a roadmap to that future. But your vision must also lead to a better future for them, not just for your company. By tying your vision to the better future each individual needs, you gain commitment where others would require compliance. As a leader, you are responsible for helping each person find their way to their vision.
- **Recognize status roles.** Certain status roles move individuals toward or away from enrollment. When someone sees enroll-ment as affirming or providing them with a higher status role,

they will be more inclined or motivated to enroll. Those who believe enrollment threatens their status role may avoid enrollment to maintain that status. You must inspire those who see themselves leveling up by enrolling, while also ensuring that enrolling enables doubters to maintain or improve their status.

- **See and acknowledge fears.** People always worry about change, even positive change. Their worries may include not being ready, not being good enough, or simply letting people down. Your role as the leader is to assuage their fears. Just like a prospective client can't move forward until you help them resolve their concerns, those with unaddressed fears may struggle to enroll. Let them know you'll be there for them when they need you.

- **Invite them to an adventure.** We sometimes get change initiatives wrong, especially when we treat change only as fixing a problem. While that might be true, highlighting a problem is not the best strategy for winning hearts and minds. Your invitation is to an adventure, one that will provide new experiences and a chance to blaze a new trail. An adventure is better than the status quo, and it can increase engagement. After all, good leaders are unfaithful to the status quo.

- **Create compelling experiences to begin the journey.** To make your vision attractive, you need to start with experiences that encourage team members to take the first step: a planning meeting, a special training, or something else to get your team interested and excited. Whether you start by sharing your vision or invite your team to a Future Now Workshop to build a plan to create a new future state, a concrete experience is much more interactive (and effective) than a long email calling for compliance.

- **Initiate them into the tribe.** There is a common factor in those who choose to enroll: the desire to belong to something bigger than themselves. Every tribe has an initiation. These ceremonies help new members break from the past as they begin a new journey and build a new identity. One way to approach that task is to require a test that team members must complete to enjoy initiation into the tribe.

- **Instill the mission with meaning and contribution.** Enrollment requires meaning and the chance to contribute to something bigger than oneself. Revenue growth may inspire you, and you and your team may have incentives should you succeed. But you will find fewer people motivated by money than by the chance to do good work. You must provide the individuals you invite to enroll with a vision that provides meaning and purpose so you can speak to values higher than money alone. Your appeal should stress the value you create for others and how you contribute to your team's success by helping your clients succeed.

- **Share how enrollees will grow and what it will mean.** In any great story, the protagonist is unprepared to accept their call, but they always find their Yoda, someone to teach them what they need to succeed in their mission. Whenever you transform your team and the individuals who comprise it, you prepare them to tackle even more difficult outcomes. No person should be the same as when you started the transformation. They should all grow.

- **Focus on creating commitment.** There is a major shift in your leadership when you ask your enrollees to commit to change. Mostly, your enrollees have been asked to comply, a lesser commitment that leaves room for the status quo. A commitment to change is much more powerful than doing something just because it is expected of you. Get this right and you improve accountability.

- **Feed the soul of those who enroll.** Each person who enrolls in your change needs you to feed their soul. In other words, you must communicate your vision in a way that provides them what they need, including the affirmation and encouragement

that what they do makes things better for other people, something most leaders leave unaddressed.

- **Make it bigger on the inside.** Enrollment changes you from an
  outsider to an insider, so you have to make life bigger on the
  inside. Joining a group of people working to improve their results
  and make a difference is better than simply going through the
  motions, making their calls, updating their CRM, and so on.
- **Create leaders that inspire others to enroll and transform.**
  Leaders have followers, but they make leaders. When you enroll
  people in your vision, you create and build future leaders, ones
  who can inspire others to enroll. Your legacy will not be revenue
  growth, even though you might shatter the record for greatest
  increase in a calendar year. It will be the leaders who grew under
  your leadership and are now prepared to do the same for others.

## Your Revenue Growth Goal

We can't leave this chapter without doing the work to establish your
revenue growth goal. Here's the revenue growth formula you need:

$$\text{Existing Revenue} - \text{Churn} + \text{Net New Revenue} = \text{Growth}$$

Let's assume your goal is 12 percent growth year over year.
Let's say your last year's revenue was $12,000,000, but you know
that you will lose $2,000,000 in churn. For now, don't worry about
why that revenue is gone; that's something you can work on later.
That leaves you with $10,000,000 of existing revenue. Twelve per-
cent growth means you will need $1,200,000 in net new revenue.

But let me tell you why you shouldn't target 12 percent
growth: that goal is not big enough to cause you or your team to
change in any significant way. If your goal doesn't cause you to
ask yourself, "How on earth am I am going to do that?" then it's
not big enough. Missing a 25 percent growth goal and coming

in at 19 percent instead is better than the 12 percent you might have settled for, had you not raised your goal. One sales organization I know wanted to add 10 percent growth on top of their existing $10,000,000 existing revenue. I suggested they shoot for $20,000,000. They missed the goal but came in at $17,000,000.

Eventually, your vision will include a list of outcomes that ensure you reach your goal, along with the changed beliefs and behaviors that will create the opportunities you need to meet new, aggressive, and somewhat scary goals. Let's go!

# 2

# Transformation

A TRANSFORMATION IS a "burn the boats on the shoreline" kind of change. It's not an incremental change. It's a revolutionary change, one that suggests the past is no more. When you remove the possibility of going back to the status quo, you eliminate everything but the future.

Your vision is the starting point of your transformation and your path to revenue growth. There are two reasons these transformations are necessary. In some cases, a transformative change initiative is necessary because a sales team is failing and needs to change what they are doing to improve their results. But more often, a sales leader decides to pursue a transformation because they recognize their team has latent potential that will unlock even better outcomes. In both cases, the only way your results change is if you lead your team by articulating and applying your transformative vision.

Transformations are never easy and rarely rapid, movie montages notwithstanding. Transformation isn't something you do by providing your team an email about the change you want or a training program to improve your team's ability to make a cold call, neither of which is likely to drive the behavioral changes necessary to go from good to great to exceptional. In Chapter 1, we looked at resistance to change and several strategies to enroll your team in your vision. By all means, devote your time and energy to inviting people to join the adventure and be part of something big. But no matter how well you enroll your team and work through constructive tension and positive friction, you will still face resistance from certain cynics, skeptics, and potential holdouts.

## Barriers to Transformation

You probably already know who will resist your vision. However, a successful transformation is only possible when leaders insist that each person on their team makes the changes that result in better results and greater revenue growth. To avoid letting these naysayers win, watch out for these barriers to effective transformation.

- **A Lack of Managerial Will.** Make no mistake: no matter how positive you are about your transformation, it is still a battle of wills. Good leadership includes the managerial will to lead your team and your refusal to allow anyone in your sales force to usurp that role. Losing a battle of wills, even over something small, is likely to make your transformation wither on the vine.
- **Making Exceptions.** You likely have several successful, strong-willed employees who will argue that their results should exempt them from participating in your transformation. Don't believe them. Allowing anyone to opt out of your change initiative will cause others to believe that your transformation is optional. It must be mandatory.
- **The Strong Pull of Habit.** When a person has done something in the same way for a long time, the pull of habit is difficult to resist. A transformation requires removing old habits that prevent your team from growing your revenue with new habits that ensure you achieve your revenue goals.
- **Distractions and Lack of Focus.** I recently watched two large sales organizations pull their whole sales force out of the field to implement training and onboarding for Salesforce.com. Every second they spent on this administrative project was time away from creating and winning opportunities, something like taking your football team off the field to wash and iron everybody's uniforms.
- **No Changed Behaviors.** Most sales leaders who seek transformation want new and better results without having to hold their teams accountable for changing how they act. The chance of enacting a successful transformation without changed behaviors is exactly 0.0 percent.

■ **Ending the Transformation Early.** Some sales organizations see preliminary results from a transformation and let up or wind down before they've crossed the finish line. Early success is encouraging, but the only way to be sure you've transformed is when you have your vision and have reached your revenue goal.

## Rules for Successful Transformations

Beyond avoiding these pitfalls, there are a few rules for transformations that will help ensure you succeed. Even the simple rules are difficult to maintain over time, but they are necessary. Plan to come back to this chapter after you have read this entire book, so you can troubleshoot your transformation as you go.

### *Rule 1: You Go First*

Your most important responsibility in leading your team through the transformation is being the first one to change. Chances are, you have been modeling (even unconsciously) the sales leaders who led you, rather than forming your own unique vision. But they probably never tried to enroll you in a change initiative—like you, they were just at work to work.

The more you need your team to change, the more you need to change. That starts by changing how you engage with them, including what you expect from them and the higher standards you will require. As you read through this book, you'll learn to communicate differently and use different leadership styles for different scenarios, two practices that will make your change unmistakable to everyone around you.

No one has sold their vision to others without first embracing it themselves. No great leader ever convinced others to change without first changing themselves. If you want your team to change, you must lead by example: you go first.

I once facilitated a workshop for seven hundred salespeople after delivering a keynote speech. During my keynote, the entire sales leadership team watched from the front two tables. But once the workshop started, every leader walked out of the room, en masse. I was stunned. Not only would those leaders not understand how to support their teams or what they should expect from them, but they broadcasted to all 700 salespeople that their learning wasn't important.

The best leaders I've met are even more engaged than their sales force. They lead change by example, even when they're implementing their own visions. You have a greater ability to transform your team by making the changes you need to make first.

## Rule 2: Why Comes First

I've never understood why salespeople—a group who spend much of their time helping their clients change—have such an allergy to changing themselves. Ask a hundred salespeople whether their prospective client should change to improve their results, and you'll get a hundred ayes. Ask that same group if their own companies should change, and they'll bombard you with dozens of recommendations for running things better.

But ask your team if they should individually change, and all you'll hear is excuses—or perhaps crickets. It's easy to believe that all your problems and challenges are caused by others: prospects who won't invest, clients who won't agree, competitors who won't play fair, and colleagues who won't work hard. It's more difficult to believe that you are the primary source of your own problems. The Buddhists have a saying for this: "You are perfect just the way you are, and you could use some improvement."

You will have a tough time starting your transformation without making the case for change. Your vision provides (at least) one reason to change, but there are other reasons, like the external forces that make selling more difficult, largely because decision-makers and buyers find buying more challenging. Maybe you think your results are perfect just the way they are, but you have not yet reached your full potential.

No matter what, "why change" must come before "what must change."

## Rule 3: Install New Beliefs

The word "meme" may bring to mind a funny video of a kitten climbing up curtains or a photo of a perpetually distracted boyfriend. But the term was actually coined by the evolutionary biologist Richard Dawkins, in his book *The Selfish Gene*. Dawkins argued that certain ideas spread and compete for hearts and minds, suggesting that memes, like genes, reproduce. Howard Bloom's later work in *The Lucifer Principle* suggests that the most powerful memes have a sort of self-protection mechanism, making them difficult to uninstall.

The main obstacle to installing a new set of beliefs is the assumption that what you've been doing for years or decades is good and right and true. When you answer "why change" for your sales team, the answer must suggest that while your past actions were right for their time, now you need to change to address new challenges in your industry and market. That avoids a long and unfruitful conversation about the past you are leaving behind and keeps everyone focused on future revenue.

To realize your vision, you must uninstall the past beliefs and replace them with new ones that support your goals. My sample vision in Chapter 1 includes beliefs like "We create greater value than any competitor, never needing to answer 'why us' because our sales conversations have proven we are the right choice," and "We command a price higher than our competition because we provide outcomes worth paying more to obtain." Success will elude you unless and until you install the new beliefs that underpin your transformation. They form the very heart and soul of your journey to revenue growth.

## Rule 4: New Outcomes Need New Actions

The heart of a transformation is built on new outcomes and the new actions your sales team is going to take to produce them. The outcomes you need may be exclusive to you, but if you want revenue growth, you need two primary outcomes: (1) creating more new opportunities that result in net new revenue, and (2) winning more of those opportunities to deliver new revenue. The actions may include more prospecting activity, a more effective sales approach, and for your part as the leader, deeper engagement with your team.

Changing hearts and minds is important, but the core of your transformation is new actions and new outcomes. There is no way to produce new results without new actions and outcomes, including a significant increase in the fundamental activities that produce revenue growth. The greatest amount of your time and energy in a transformation should go toward teaching, training, encouraging, coaching, and requiring new behaviors, or more of the right actions.

The challenge is preventing individual salespeople from going right back to doing what they've always done. You will need to ensure your team is doing what's new instead of what's comfortable. Without new activities, you won't produce the new outcomes or reach your targets.

Highlight these new activities by changing your CRM's dashboard, prioritizing the new activities you need from your team and the outcomes of those activities. This is especially important if you are adopting a new, modern sales approach to replace an outdated legacy approach. Similarly, recognize and praise those who are doing the real work of the transformation, which encourages others to do the same.

These behavioral changes will make or break your transformation, even as they make it much more challenging to reach your goals. For many sales leaders, the most important new actions are: (1) prospecting, and (2) avoiding transactional "opportunities" that show up as unsolicited requests for proposal. But many others need to change how their salespeople pursue opportunities, something we'll cover later in Chapter 10 on sales effectiveness.

## Rule 5: Defend Your Transformation

Transformation comes with risks, including the risk that some of your salespeople will opt to leave your team rather than enroll in your vision. After all, a transformation means more work to go along with the changed beliefs and new actions. You may have a salesperson or two who decides the grass is greener across the street, even if they don't realize that your competitor (and their new boss) has had higher standards and greater expectations for some time. But no matter why people leave, you can be sure that anyone who doesn't want to change will not be much help to you. Sometimes it's better for an individual or a clique to leave than to stay and actively work against your vision.

You may likewise be challenged in a public forum, in which case you must defend your vision there and then. You must allow no challenge to go unanswered, no matter who delivers the attack. There is no appeasement, no negotiation, and no promising to have a private conversation later. The best approach is to address any challenge immediately and directly. Any hesitation or avoidance will cause you to lose credibility, which means you must be able to engage in conflict politely and professionally.

In defense of your vision and your goals, here's some language you can use: "I have already made the decision that this is our way forward, and while I am always willing to listen to how we can improve this plan, I will not entertain any debate about the direction we are taking or what we need to do." In Chapter 4,

I will introduce you to several leadership styles you will need to say the words above with confidence and conviction.

You may also find that a small and quiet contingent decides to sabotage your transformation in dark corners, whispering to others that they should just "wait this out." When you hear about such mutiny, and you will, you will have to address the ringleaders. Anyone who undermines your initiative must agree to stop sowing seeds of dissent or leave your team.

I hope you have no resistance, but it's my job to make sure you know what you're up against. There is no reason to keep a salesperson who will not contribute to your vision, and even less reason to keep any individual actively working against you.

## Rule 6: Change Fast

To ensure you succeed, don't gingerly wade into change. Once you've decided, there is no turning back.

As a teenager, my friends and I would spend a lot of time camping and canoeing. Invariably, at some point someone would tip the canoe over, launching everyone into the water. Rather than anxiously awaiting the day's dunking, I got into the habit of tipping us over within the first two minutes. Once everyone was wet, we could move on.

The faster you pursue your transformation, the greater your chances of success. Allowing it to drag on threatens your results. You are better off throwing people into the deep water and getting them moving than letting them avoid change. Nobody calls "part in" at the poker table—you are all in, or all out.

As the leader, you want to control the tempo, making change fast. You may not remember that Blockbuster tried to keep their brick-and-mortar stores and slowly add an online presence. Because they hedged, they moved slowly, and soon they stopped moving at all. If you still have a VHS tape you didn't return, you no longer have to worry about late fees.

## Rule 7: Resolve to Succeed

Throughout this conversation about your vision and your transformation, we've tackled the very real chance that some of your team will reject your vision and the transformation that will deliver the results you need. So be it: you are the leader, and it is your vision. You must resolve to succeed.

There is likely to be a battle of wills with employees who don't want to change. Your resolve must be greater than your opposition. There is every reason to engage with those who have something positive to contribute to your vision and your plan to execute it. But it is a mistake to entertain any opposition once you have decided to transform.

One option is to engage those who are likely to reject change by asking them to participate as leaders in this transformation, provided they have the right competencies and the right attitude. If this is not possible, then you may have to sit down with them and explain that you expect them to support your initiative—and that you are resolved to make the change, with or without them.

If you lose the battle of wills, you lose your vision. Later, we will look at how to make difficult decisions that prevent problems growing revenue.

## Rule 8: Focus on Progress

One always comes before two, and two always precedes three. This is the nature of progress.

It would be wonderful to complete your transformation all at once, overhauling your entire approach and still clocking out in time for happy hour. However, transformations take time and effort, even if you make changes quickly. The leader who looks for perfection, or even near-perfection, is certain to be disappointed. Instead of looking for perfect, focus on progress. If you see progress, things are good. When there is no progress, you will need to intervene, raise the stakes, and move people to bring the future closer by doing more or increasing their effectiveness.

At some point, you'll find yourself on a plateau, making no visible or measurable progress. You can expect to encounter several plateaus as you implement your vision. You will have to poke, prod, and press your team to keep climbing, even when the ground seems flat.

No matter how small the progress, celebrate it. Even a small result proves you are progressing, and you must recognize those successes. Take every opportunity to heap praise on the individuals with results that are improving. This will help sustain your transformation.

## Rule 9: One Thousand to One

For every thousand times you say something, you can expect exactly one action. And not even one action from each person on your team—one action total. The hyperbole is deliberate: too many sales leaders overestimate obedience when engaging in a transformation, creating a problem that must be corrected quickly. Like toddlers hoping to avoid naptime, some salespeople engage selective hearing when their sales leader communicates with them. Even if they hear the words, understand the request, and nod or even squeeze out a "yes," the result is still no behavioral change.

Don't assume that you can tell a person once what you need them to do, and they will immediately run out and do it. You must play all four quarters, continually overcommunicating the whole way (not to worry, Chapter 3 will cover this in detail). In other words, the action you need to take here is never to stop communicating what you want and need from your sales force.

*Rule 10: Resetting Your Relationship with Your Team*

Before we move forward to some sample language, we need to deal with one more important rule for your transformation: enacting your vision means resetting your relationship with your team. Few leaders provide their teams with the leadership they need to reach their full potential. After all, every leader has more than enough to do, including constant interruptions and more than their fair share of emergencies. You may also be the kind of person who is intrinsically motivated to work hard and be accountable for the commitments you make, so you expect your employees to behave as you would.

There is a legal defense called a waiver. Maybe you have seen the term in your contracts, in phrases like "not enforcing any of these terms is not considered a waiver." Say your client accepts your delivery every week for five years, even though it is ever so slightly out of spec. The first week of year six, they reject your delivery and refuse to pay for the shipment, arguing that it is out of spec.

You are stunned, not because the shipment was wrong but because your client accepted it for five years without a peep. Shouldn't they have said something earlier? So legally, you can argue that because your client said nothing about your out-of-spec shipments, they have waived the right to reject your delivery now. The waiver defense might win in this scenario, but it's a dangerous threat when your team uses it to reject your vision.

For example, maybe in the past you have not required your team to spend some significant time prospecting each day. You have "suggested" that they might benefit from prospecting for 90 minutes a day. You have even forwarded posts and articles from people documenting better results when salespeople block their time to prospect. And besides, your team would much rather interact on

LinkedIn or by email than pick up the phone and call a prospect. Were I the judge, I would agree that you have waived any right to be unhappy with your team for taking a lackadaisical approach to prospecting, given that you've tolerated it as long as you have.

What you need to do now is to tear up the invisible contract you have been (unknowingly) using and start with a new contract, one that will not fall so quickly to a waiver defense since no accountability will be waived in the future. To reset and restart your transformation, you will have to take full responsibility in public and establish a new set of standards and accountabilities. Here's some sample language to get you started with that communication.

**A Working Script**   First, I want to say I'm sorry. As your leader, I have failed you by not creating a set of standards that would allow us to reach our full potential as a team or ensuring each person reaches their full potential here. I apologize for not being as engaged as I should have in certain aspects of your development, and for paying too much attention to internal needs instead. Going forward, I will do better.

While we have a lot of strengths, we have not always capitalized on them. We also have several glaring problems to address with some urgency, especially when it comes to the time we spend prospecting, the number of opportunities we create, and the number of deals that stall, die of old age, or simply disappear without a trace. Leaving these deals in our pipeline has given us a false sense of security and prevented us from going out to create and win more deals.

Starting today, we will begin a transformation. It's going to be an adventure, and all of us are going to have to grow and develop, a process that I have already started. We will transform from being a good team to being the best sales team in the company. As part of this transformation, we're also going to become the most effective sales force in the industry.

I am asking you to enroll in this transformation. I want you to commit to the changes we need to make, and I am going to give you my own commitment to help you in every way I can. With that in mind, I want to share with you my vision for this team.

## Next Steps

At that point, of course, you will have to give your team your unique vision and explain the changes you will need to help them make. You have set the stage by taking responsibility for the past and starting a conversation about what comes next. The remainder of this book will provide you with strategies that will ensure you succeed—provided you and your team do the work.

# 3

## Communication

You're busy running a sales team and racing toward your goals, which means spending most days talking to senior leaders, your sales team, important clients and prospects, and the rest of your organization. It feels like you are always communicating in one medium or another—talking, typing, asking or answering questions, and providing or receiving information.

But all that communication may be doing little to promote revenue growth. Communicating for revenue growth requires a different approach, with more direct conversations that carry more information. Bringing your vision to life, enrolling your team in an adventure, and successfully transforming your team and your results requires more of the right communication.

As a sales leader, I never stop telling my team, "Go acquire anchor clients." I never miss an opportunity to tell my team what I want from them, even though they have heard me say "anchor clients" hundreds or thousands of times. You might call these key accounts, dream clients, must-win, high-visibility, high-value, or some other moniker—they're the kind of clients you can create significant value for and who believe the outcomes you can help them improve are strategic. Growing these larger clients adds more to your numbers than growing smaller clients, especially when the smaller clients don't consider what you sell to be particularly vital to their work.

## What We Value and Why

More broadly, your communication must convey what you value and why it's important. Because you have told your team what you want, you may feel they already know what you value and why. You may think you have conveyed the message effectively, but constant communication shows that your priorities are still priorities—and that they're not going to change.

A lot of sales forces suffer from too much communication about too many projects, and the sheer volume might cause them to believe that there are other priorities above—or at least equal to—yours. There is research that suggests that the average knowledge worker receives 127 emails every day and sends 40, numbers so large that most emails can hardly be called communication, let alone communication that leads to revenue growth. I know you can't stop the rest of your company from distracting your sales force with messages that take time away from growing revenue. But you can (and must) communicate so it drowns out as much of the distractions and attention diverters as possible, redirecting your team toward what you value and telling them why.

## How We Win and Succeed

There are a lot of ways to teach, train, and develop a sales force. Whether your team still needs to transform or has already done so, your communication must convey how you intend to win deals and how the individuals on your team will succeed. In a later chapter we'll take a deeper dive into the strategy specifics, but for now you need to know that every conversation offers you a chance to transmit and transfer what your team needs to do to create and win new opportunities and clients.

Communicating how you win might sound like this: "We win when we create greater value than any of our competitors through our insight-based sales approach and provide better counsel, advice, and recommendations inside the conversations we have with our clients. We succeed when we play our game without any concern for what our competition does or doesn't do."

The first time you say something like this, those who aren't yet convinced you're right will be incredulous, believing instead that whatever they have done before will enable them to win and succeed now. A few will hang on to the idea that external factors like pricing determine whether they win or lose deals, no matter what they do. But the more you repeat this message, the more you will convert the unconverted. Eventually, they'll recognize what you say is true, but not if you stop saying it.

Leading growth means ruthlessly prioritizing the very things that result in net new revenue: creating new opportunities and winning enough of those opportunities to hit your growth targets. Any time you stop conveying what you value and why, along with how you expect your team to win and reach their goals, you will find that a significant number of your salespeople will ease up on the activities that produce your desired results.

You may worry about repeating yourself, but chasing revenue means you likely haven't been saying enough of these things—or saying them often enough. Besides, the more deeply you understand your vision and your goals, the more ways you'll find to explain what and how to win.

One day, I was on a flight with the CEO and founder of one of my clients, en route to speak to one of his teams. We had spoken together several times, and we both knew each other's favorite talking points. On the flight, he turned and said, "You know, I keep saying the same thing every time I speak. Should I change what I am saying?" I told him he should never change his message, as doing so would confuse his converts and believers. But I did advise him to keep the message fresh: "Change the stories, change the data, and change the examples."

What you say is true until you stop saying it. To communicate the same vision over time, you need to find ways to provide variety while still staying on message. There are at least four components you can vary: data, stories, trends, and actions. Let's start with data.

## What the Data Tells Us

There has never been a time where it was so easy to generate and access so much data. The data you use is an important component of any communication. For example, imagine you have challenged your sales team to increase their prospecting efforts. Your data may show that your team set a record for new meetings. It might also show that your team showed no improvement.

Data is powerful because it speaks the truth. Data is not an opinion, making it impervious to arguments, and it doesn't change its mind. Data illuminates inconvenient truths, providing a strong dose of reality. It's important that you use data, particularly sales math, because revenue growth is a number, made up of leading indicators that allow you to quantify your wins and losses.

## Tell Me a Story

Ever since we started painting cave walls, humans have been storytellers. Stories are valuable because they provide handles, making it easy to transfer the lesson to others. But even more than their portability, stories also provide an understanding of our world. The more you pay attention to the stories that surround you and the ones you hear from your sales team, the greater your repertoire. Stories about individuals on your team are interesting to other people. Even if a few employees get jealous or cynical when you tell a story about a colleague's success, they will remember the story.

Collecting stories not only provides the ability to teach something important, but they reinforce core values, entertain your team, and allow you to make a point about what's important and why. Your stories might also explain why someone lost a deal, a story best told by the person who suffered the loss, with some ideas about what they would do differently.

## Connect Your Communication to Trends

At the time I am writing this section of the book, Russia has invaded Ukraine, inflation is at a 40-year high, oil is just over $115 a barrel, there is still a computer chip shortage, and supply chain issues are slowing everything down. At the same time, masses of people are quitting their jobs (the Great Resignation), leaving ten million open jobs in the United States with too few people to fill them.

When you can tie your vision to the context of the day's events and the trend lines those events disclose, you create a sense of why your team must change, why your clients must change, and the difference your team can make for people struggling to produce the results they need. A side benefit of communicating around the trends and happenings in the business world is that your team will steal your talk tracks and potentially become interested in improving their business acumen.

## What Action You Need from Your Team

Every communication should remind your team of what they need to do, why they need to do it, and how it contributes to their overall success. For example: (1) create more new opportunities, (2) plan your sales calls, and (3) facilitate your buyer's journey by providing your clients with advice on how to pursue the change they need to make. And if not for my publication deadline and a pesky 65,000-word limit, I would list a hundred other actions and explain why each one is important, but I trust you can identify them because you know your team. If you need more help, go to www.thesalesblog.com/leadinggrowth.

For now, please allow me to offer you strong direction about FYI (For Your Information) or CYA (Cover Your Ass) communications: avoid any message that doesn't require your team to act or reinforce an important, continuing outcome you need from them. The memo about new logo colors can wait, even if you are elated the new color is Fuchsia.

In my note-taking application, I collate links to articles that improve my ability to tell a story, share data, and share the implications of trends. To execute constant communication, you must always collect new source material. Every conversation with a salesperson gives you a potential story to share, especially if it helps you communicate your vision, your goals, and why they're both important for your team, your clients, and your company.

## Nine Primary Leadership Communications

There are many questions your team needs you to answer for them. They may not ask these questions out loud, but the absence of a question doesn't mean it doesn't exist, let alone that your team already knows the answer. Every question a salesperson asks you is something you can share with the rest of your force. Besides, chances are good that someone else has been wondering the same thing, even if they are too timid to ask you directly. The more you answer questions using the components here, the better and the more powerful your communication.

To make this practical and tactical, let's next look at the nine most important types of leadership communications. These fall into four categories: vision, expectations and accountability, execution, and the individual. These questions can prime your sales team to make changes and pursue revenue growth. When your team members lack strong direction, they wonder and wander. You don't want to wait for individuals to ask you these questions or any of their derivations. Instead, proactively answer them to maintain enrollment and increase confidence.

| Area of Focus | Questions |
|---|---|
| Vision | 1. Where are you leading us?<br>2. Why are we pursuing this path? |
| Expectations and Accountability | 3. What do you expect of me?<br>4. What will be different now? |
| Execution | 5. How do we succeed?<br>6. How do we overcome these obstacles?<br>7. How are we doing? |
| Individual | 8. What's in it for me?<br>9. Why does my individual contribution matter? |

## Question 1: Where Are You Leading Us?

The reason this book starts with vision is because without one, you cannot answer this first and fundamental question. Without a vision of the future results, you make it more difficult to lead your team, and with no goal, there's no North Star to guide and pull your team forward.

No coach starts their season by telling their team, "Let's work really hard, play some games, and we'll see what happens." They start the season explaining how they will improve and how they can make it to the National Championship. Your North Star must explain how your team will transform and how that will lead your revenue growth.

There should never be a week where you don't communicate your vision and your revenue goals. When you stop consistently communicating your vision, your team is all but certain to let up (even if they don't mean to), costing you time and requiring the next-to-impossible task of restarting your transformation.

## Question 2: Why Are We Pursuing This Path?

For a team to change, they need clear reasons. The better the reasons, the greater your chances of getting the buy-in and the behavioral changes necessary to move you toward your revenue goals. Maybe you want your team to be the most successful team when measured by net new revenue. Or you might want your team to have the highest percentage growth, something that will naturally result in revenue growth. With a goal and a vision, you turn individuals into a team.

With your goal and your vision in place, you have a reason to change: "To reach our goals and become the team with the highest percentage growth, we are going to have to create and win more opportunities. Without those opportunities, we won't be able to be the fastest growing sales team."

There is no end of answers to "why change," including something as simple as the goal and vision of having the highest growth rate. You might also lean on your team's potential, outlining what everyone must do to contribute to the goal. This approach allows you to speak to individuals about their contribution to the effort.

These first two communications, "where you are leading us," and "why you are pursuing this path," are core conversations. There are more questions you need to answer, but these two must always be front and center.

## Question 3: What Do You Expect of Me?

People do better when they know exactly what is expected of them. The greater clarity around what is expected of each member of your team, the better your results. Expectations set up accountability. As you pursue net new revenue growth, you will need to increase your expectations.

Please remember the revenue growth formula:

$$\text{Existing Revenue} - \text{Churn} + \text{Net New Revenue}$$

To increase your revenue, you must demand more won opportunities and more new clients. Your team will need to spend more time prospecting and scheduling new meetings, including the senior salespeople whom you may have allowed to live on their existing clients. You also need your sales force to create new opportunities with their existing clients.

Because there is no way to grow revenue without creating and winning new opportunities, you would do well to continually communicate that need, something we'll cover in greater detail in later chapters. Here, you might also have to require that your sales team change their sales approach if you need to increase their individual and collective sales effectiveness.

## Question 4: What Will Be Different Now?

Communicating what will be different speaks to your new expectations moving forward. If the question "What do you expect from me?" clarifies the outcomes you need from your team, this one speaks to the specific activities you need them to do.

Here it is best to link actions to outcomes, like "doubling the number of meetings we have each week," "prospecting for 90 minutes each day to gain those meetings," "creating more new, large client opportunities," or "changing our approach to a modern, insight-based conversation to create greater value." These details help you and your team recognize the specific activities and results they need to create.

## Question 5: How Do We Succeed?

I struggle when a sales leader sets a goal like "increase our pipeline by 8X" or "double our revenue in the next 12 months without adding to the size of our sales force." What bothers me is not the lofty ambition but that the leaders never explain exactly how they will create these miracles. As far as I can tell, the Gods of Sales don't hear the prayers of sales leaders and salespeople who aren't doing the right work.

Any outcome you expect your team to deliver must come with directions on how they can achieve the result. The expectation that each person on your team must prospect for 90 minutes each day may be enough for them to double their meetings (especially if they only had one weekly meeting before). But reaching that goal might also mean changing their approach and their talk tracks, or using a prospecting cadence that uses several touches in multiple mediums.

It's important that you explain how your team will succeed. However, that doesn't mean you don't also expect them to be resourceful and to take the initiative to figure out the best way for them to succeed. If you can't even tell your team what they need to do to succeed, they'll lose all faith that they can do what you are asking of them.

## Question 6: How Do We Overcome These Obstacles?

What you are asking your team to do isn't easy. They are certain to run into obstacles along the way, both in terms of creating new opportunities and winning the opportunities that result in net new revenue. Your communication must address how to overcome these challenges as they do the work of creating revenue growth.

There are easy obstacles and challenging obstacles you will need to address. An easy obstacle might be resolving clients' concerns when the salesperson asks for a meeting. Because all the client's objections can be distilled to a single concern—"I believe this is a waste of my time"—this is a rather easy obstacle to dispatch. A more difficult obstacle is something like displacing a competitor with a must-win, high-visibility, high-value prospective client.

There will be opportunities for you to have members of your team explain how they address these obstacles, with different people sharing different tactics, giving your team options to explore besides what you teach them to do.

## Question 7: How Are We Doing?

Positive or negative, you need to communicate with your team about how they are doing. Positive results breed future positive results. Any time you have the possibility to point to positive results, you must use it to prove that what you are doing is working. The more you can share success, the more your vision becomes real. There will always be examples of your top salespeople succeeding, but you should also show success from the individuals not blessed with as much natural talent.

Negative results or no results also require communication, pointing your team back to expectations, accountabilities, and execution. When you are off-course and making no progress, you must remind your team that you have confidence in them, both as a team and as individuals. It's always best to be candid when dealing with negative results. Coating bad results with sugar isn't the right way to approach poor results, but neither is being angry or upset.

People want to know where they are and how they are doing. Make progress reports frequently and track your progress toward your vision.

## Question 8: What's in It for Me?

You don't have to always address "what's in it for me" with every individual. Instead, you can address the benefits of your vision and revenue growth to your entire team. Some small percent-age of your sales force will be motivated by money. Another seg-ment will be motivated by recognition. Still another part will be pulled toward doing work that provides purpose and meaning. And there are some who just need to feel they belong.

Because you have a vision, you can explain how pursuing the path you have them on can result in more money, greater recog-nition, doing meaningful work, and belonging to a team going somewhere. It's important to know what motivates each member of your team, especially when you speak to them as individuals. Tell people how they will grow and improve, reenrolling them in your vision and the adventure you are leading.

## Question 9: Why Does My Individual Contribution Matter?

To create revenue growth, you need every person on your team to contribute to your results. If only 5 people in a sales force con-tribute to revenue growth, it doesn't matter whether the roster lists 8 or 80. In particular, senior reps who are coasting on the annuities from their largest accounts, without creating any new net revenue, need to understand why their individual contribu-tion matters.

Every salesperson needs to contribute something to revenue growth. No one should be allowed to opt out, and no one should be allowed to fail without being provided the support they need to make some meaningful contribution.

## How to Repeat Yourself Without Saying the Same Thing

Using only the four variables of data, story, trend, and action, you can create unlimited communications, as you need not change every element. Let's say you want to speak about why your vision is important and why the sales force needs to change. Maybe you start Week 1 by using elements A, B, C, D. When you come back to this topic in Week 5 you present elements A, E, C, F, changing the data and the story, but keeping the trend and the required action. At the start of a new quarter, you stress A, G, H, I. With a stack of index cards and a decent gel pen, like the Pilot G2, you can easily keep track of your content, selecting just the right combination for every communication.

The nine questions listed above provide you with even more ways to convey your priorities without it feeling repetitive, even though you are saying the same thing in a new way. Those who have trouble grasping one combination often resonate with another one, and those who get confused by directions might do much better with stories. Everything you see and hear is potential communication fodder, if you do the work of capturing it and matching it to your vision. Now you know how I've been publishing daily blog posts for more than a decade!

Finally, remember that there is never a bad time to remind your team about your vision, especially since most leaders don't talk about it enough. When your team or several salespeople are succeeding, share that success with the rest of the team, offering social proof that your vision is both possible and beneficial. At the end of the day, all you're doing is approaching every conversation as an opportunity to speak to revenue growth. Using data, stories, trends, and action effectively can infect your team with the idea that revenue growth is important to you, and because that's true, it must be important to them as well.

# PART

# II

# Taking the Lead

IN THIS PART, we are going to explore three areas of focus, starting with the value of applying the right leadership style to the right scenario. From there, we'll discuss how to make decisions that lead to revenue growth—a central part of leading growth, and one of the most challenging. Then we'll discuss strategy and alignment, meaning how to make sure everyone on your team is doing what's required to achieve your vision for growth. All three of these, if not successfully addressed, can prevent revenue.

# 4

## Leadership Styles

PART OF LEADING growth is understanding when your team needs something different from you to secure their best performance. In fact, one reason sales leaders fail to grow revenue is that they only lead with their default style.

To be the leader your team needs, you must use several leadership styles, including some that don't come naturally to you. Because most sales leaders use a democratic, consensus-building style, we'll start there, but then consider six other approaches that are often necessary in certain scenarios. Later in this chapter, we'll look at a prospecting problem and how to use different strategic styles to match the nature of the problem.

## The Democratic Consensus-Builder

You want to be a good leader and help your team bring your vision to life, exceeding all expectations and growing your revenue. But you also want your team to like and respect you, so you are approachable, positive, encouraging, and always willing to engage your team in new initiatives, working to get their buy-in. If this describes you, it's likely that you have a democratic, consensus-building leadership style. That style certainly has its advantages, but not every scenario rewards that type of leadership.

Focusing on likability and consensus will not necessarily help your team succeed beyond what they thought was possible. No one longs for the good old days when their boss neglected them, recognized how limited they were, and allowed them to be mediocre. Instead, the leaders they tell stories about are the ones who engaged with them, recognized their potential, and pushed them to reach their potential, even when they resisted.

The democratic leadership style, like all the other choices available, has many favorable qualities and outcomes. Notably, it creates a higher level of engagement than many other styles. This engagement helps you enroll your team in your vision,

67

encouraging them to commit and not just comply. By allowing your salespeople to help design their own plans and giving them the autonomy to try things they believe will help them succeed, you get greater commitment than if you just tell them what to do, with no chance to shape the standards for their own accountability.

But there is a downside to a democratic leadership style: some salespeople treat commands as suggestions, especially when there was no unanimous agreement to operate a certain way. Even when your conversations are polite and professional, these salespeople will often fall back on their preferences instead of your vision. When that's the case, you will encounter two problems that prevent revenue growth. First, some team members will decide to "wait you out" instead of taking some important new action. They often learn this behavior from watching past initiatives wither and die—one of the oldest games in the world—especially if they see you take a wait-and-see approach to your own leaders' directives.

To compound that problem, the salespeople who avoid necessary change are often also the ones who work to bring people over to their side, showing that it's safe to go back to the way things were done before you decided to transform your team and your results. When you allow the holdouts to go unaddressed, this belief that no one must change metastasizes, creating greater harm to the sales force and threatening your revenue growth.

Other leadership styles can easily overcome the resistance to change, but use them wisely—they rarely work well as your default style.

## The Autocratic Style

The autocrat is everything that the democratic leader is not. The autocrat doesn't particularly care whether they are liked, even though they often feign friendship with their employees. They are rarely capable of being sincerely positive or encouraging, so they have little interest in winning hearts and minds. There is, however, a certain value wrapped up in the autocratic approach.

Let me begin with a disclaimer. I'm not suggesting that you become a full-time autocrat, placing a picture of Joseph Stalin next to the one of your significant other and your children. And trust me, and skip the bushy moustache. Nor should you lead through fear, the primary strategy of the autocratic leader. The autocrat uses their formal power instead of inspiration, moral authority, or persuasion. Blunt force is the strategy of "leaders" incapable of influence and true leadership.

That said, it's not only necessary but healthy to occupy the role of autocrat when it is necessary. Don't believe me? What would you do with a salesperson who offers to pay the client a kickback to win their business? How about a salesperson who pads their expense report?

The autocrat has less trouble with the salesperson who endeavors to wait them out, but you'll pay too high a price if you adopt autocracy as your primary leadership style. For one thing, your team will suffer from high attrition. The people who do stay and work for an autocrat fear the job market more than they fear their leader. But more importantly, the best you can hope for here is compliance. Autocrats may get obedience, but they aren't going to get the best performance out of their team.

An effective leader can shift into an autocratic style for the few nonnegotiable outcomes they must defend when it comes to protecting revenue growth and their values. You might start by saying, "I understand this is new and that it isn't something you were required to do in the past. But this is so important to our results that you must do it. I am afraid this isn't something we are going to change. It's nonnegotiable. I am happy to give you additional help if you need it." You can insist that your team does what's necessary without resorting to force, threats, or power. But to do that, you need the will of the autocrat, never giving up or backing down.

## The Laissez-Faire Leader

I must confess that my default leadership style is laissez-faire, which means "hands off," or not interfering. Because I have never had to have someone tell me what to do, I used to believe that everyone worked like me. My default style caused me no end of problems as a young sales leader. To ensure I didn't have to lead my team, I hired people with years of experience and paid them incredibly well, only to discover that they needed the same leadership as new salespeople without industry experience. It was one of my biggest mistakes as a leader.

There are certainly positive outcomes from a laissez-faire style of leadership. First, you provide your team with a great deal of autonomy, freeing them up to explore, try new things, and generally direct themselves. Self-starters need little direction, so they thrive under a "hands-off" leader. So do mature, effective salespeople who are already highly motivated and disciplined.

But there are also downsides to this approach. You may allow people on your team to fail because you don't intervene in time to help them succeed. Every sales force has a few salespeople who love the autonomy but lack the discipline to do the work they need to do when it needs to be done. Later, in Chapter 7, we'll explore accountability, including how to put guardrails around salespeople, intervening while there is still time to help them succeed.

By now, I hope you are catching on to the main point of this chapter: you have different leadership styles available, all of them useful when used with the right person in the right scenario.

These same leadership styles are awful when used with the wrong person at the wrong time. It's your job to recognize how and why different people on your team need different approaches at different times.

## The Strategic Leader

When I ask sales leaders to disclose their leadership style, maybe 6 percent of each group are natural strategic leaders, though a lot more say that they would like to be more strategic.

The strategic leader operates on the border between their company's ongoing operations and the potential growth opportunities available to them. A strategic leader can recognize the strategies and tactics necessary to produce better results, often teaching, training, and coaching their team to improve their effectiveness. Because much of sales leadership is solving problems, the strategic leader is often the first to recognize a change is needed and to design new strategies and tactics.

The strategic leader also has a downside: sometimes, the sales force just isn't ready for what the strategic leader is asking them to do. Their strategic nature also finds these leaders with more ideas than they can execute, causing their team to lose focus. Being distracted by multiple goals and strategies, even good ones, can have a negative impact on revenue growth.

Still, when you're challenged to generate revenue growth, you must adopt the strategic leadership style: changing what needs to change, improving what needs to be improved, and conquering the obstacles to growth.

## The Bureaucratic Leader

Bureaucracy is one of the least inspiring of all the leadership styles. My strong libertarian tendencies cause me to resent compliance for compliance's sake. It might also account for how revolting I find all administrative tasks. Just looking at a form causes me to break out in hives, struggle to breathe, and on rare occasions collapse on my office floor in violent convulsions.

There are good reasons to include some bureaucracy in your leadership, especially when you work in industries like finance or healthcare where you must follow laws, rules, and guidelines—and where coloring outside the lines is often punished swiftly. But as with autocracy, you can adopt the bureaucratic style without the bureaucratic persona. Even though most sales leaders don't like to nag their sales force to do banal administrative tasks like turning in their expense reports, sometimes the nagging is necessary.

It's helpful to be able to adopt the bureaucrat style, for example, when opportunities are not properly captured in your CRM. You need to know what your pipeline looks like, and that requires data on the number and value of your potential deals. The downside of being a bureaucrat is that you must continually ask your team to put cover sheets on their TPS reports (see the movie *Office Space*), something you can promise to avoid if they promise to do the work before you have to ask.

## The Transactional Leader

The previous leadership choices have a fairly clear balance of benefits and dangers. But I've got to be honest: there isn't much of an upside to being a transactional sales leader.

Some leaders see their relationship with their sales force in purely transactional terms. The leader asks their team to do something in exchange for money. When they need the sales force to tackle the next initiative, they promise some pecuniary reward. This approach mistakenly assumes that every salesperson is money-motivated, something that just isn't true. According to Investopedia, to be in the top 5 percent of income in the United States, you need to make $342,987 annually. The top 10 percent earn at least $173,136. Let's assume that everyone in the top 10 percent is motivated by money.

That means the other 90 percent value other things more than money, and most of them sleep just fine at night.

You need look no further than your team's commission report to recognize that most salespeople don't take advantage of the unlimited potential earnings available to them. Instead, they reach a level of income that is comfortable, then try to maintain it. Despite this reality, the transactional leader believes they can buy the results they need, a theory proven wrong in every sales organization in which it is tried. While there is nothing wrong with paying for performance, you need to build in broader appeal to your initiatives to grow your revenue.

## The Transformational Leader

Some leaders are adept at helping individuals and companies transform. A leader with this natural style will expect their team to work outside of their comfort zone and move toward their potential. One of the most positive attributes of these leaders is their ability to see something in individuals they can't yet see themselves. This sometimes ends in disappointment for the leader, because nothing is more frustrating than wanting something for someone that they don't want for themselves.

Every leader needs to be able to enact this style, because every leader is leading a transformation from their current state to the better future state and their revenue growth goals. After all, this book is a guide to transforming your sales force and your results. One easy mistake to make, though, is not giving people time to integrate the changes they have made before you start the process over again. Even You 2.0 will need some time to work out some bugs.

## Providing the Right Leadership During Prospecting

You will need all seven of these leadership approaches to execute your transformation. Choose among them based on two factors:

the scenario to which you are responding, and what the individual or team needs from you to achieve their goals. Matching the right approach to the right scenario, while meeting the right needs, provides good leadership and an improvement in results. To make this concrete, let's explore the critical outcome of prospecting and creating new opportunities, matching each leadership approach to its outcome.

## Territory and Account Plans: Democratic

You need your team to create a territory and account plan for the quarter. You want them to make good decisions about which current accounts they believe they can grow by creating new opportunities. You also want them to call their own shots when it comes to winning new logos (new clients). When reviewing a salesperson's plan for the next 90 days, you notice there are a couple of prospective clients that don't show up on the rep's plan.

A good choice here is to be a democratic consensus-builder: work with the salesperson to agree on a revised plan, explaining why you believe the additional prospects are important. By allowing your team to build their own plan, you increase their engagement and commitment because it's their plan, not one you are imposing on them.

To execute that plan, in turn, each salesperson must prospect and schedule new meetings. The greatest threat to revenue growth is a lack of opportunities, something that can be solved only by prospecting.

## Prospecting Daily: Autocratic

The primacy of opportunity creation cannot be denied. Revenue growth comes from prospecting and scheduling meetings with clients and prospects. You've asked your team to block out time, to use an effective prospecting sequence, and to prioritize opportunities that result in growth. But still, they don't do enough prospecting to create the opportunities they need to reach their goals.

Even though it is an unpopular choice, you need to be a benevolent dictator when it comes to creating new opportunities weekly. You can be professional and kind while still demanding that your team prospect. Could you get the same outcome with a different approach? Yes, but I don't allow any slack around prospecting, because too much damage follows when a group of salespeople believes prospecting is optional.

## Dealing with Problems: Strategic

As you monitor your team's results, you notice they are putting forth the effort but not generating the number of quality meetings they need. Something has changed, and what once worked well enough is no longer producing the right results.

This is a role for the strategic leader. For example, you might listen to their sales calls, looking for a hint of what's off. This practice helps you look for the root cause of the problem and identify insights and ideas that might help your team book more meetings. You can also use this data to develop a new approach, then teach, train, and rehearse with your team to ensure they have the confidence and competence to execute it.

## Updating the CRM: Bureaucratic

Your team is now creating new opportunities. They tell you about them during meetings and conversations, but they rarely get around to entering the opportunity in your CRM. Without that data, you are flying blind. You've asked your team before to keep the system current, but you've seen little evidence of commitment or even compliance.

Enter the bureaucrat. The bureaucratic leader will send reminders, refuse to talk about an opportunity until it is entered in the CRM, and, if need be, make a rule that no commission will be paid on deals not in the CRM. Bureaucrats have no trouble bothering people until they comply. Resistance is futile.

## Making Change: Transformational

You've discovered that your overall sales approach is no longer producing the results it once delivered. How could what once worked so well now be the wrong choice? Well, in simple terms, the world has turned once again, and you and your team must turn with it or be left behind.

Now it's time for you and your team to transform your approach. You need to realign your approach with what your prospective clients need. More importantly, you must acquire new beliefs, new competencies, new skills, and a new approach to creating value—an approach that requires a transformational leader.

# The Empowering Recognition That Everything Is Your Fault

Even though most leaders prefer democratic consensus-building, using that leadership style exclusively will limit your effectiveness, as many scenarios are better addressed by a different approach. While no one wants to be a full-time autocrat, there are valid reasons for insisting that certain things get done in the right way and at the right time. Without an effective approach for the outcome you need from your team, you'll all struggle to produce the results that lead to incremental revenue growth.

Because you are the leader, it's important that you lead. Sometimes you can engage your team in a collaborative conversation about how to accomplish something important. In other cases, you just need them to execute with no input. No matter what, you are responsible for your team's results. Everything is your fault.

If that doesn't strike you as fair, allow me to explain. I once heard the CFO of a large and legendary company explain—live on CNBC—that the reason her company missed their quarter was because the sales force didn't hit their targets. I was aghast that a senior leader would publicly lay the blame on her sales force. Several of the company's salespeople emailed me to tell me how they felt about being thrown under the bus. To put it mildly, they were unhappy to take the brunt of the missed number.

Let's follow the trail here to discover why everything was this leader's fault. First, who was actually responsible for the sales force missing their number? According to the leader, the answer is obvious: the salespeople. But there's more going on here. To dig deeper, we need to ask a different question: Who was supposed to lead the sales force to reach their goals? Even though this makes for a more awkward talking point, it's important to recognize that the sales managers were responsible for ensuring their teams delivered on their commitments. Likewise, the company's sales leadership is responsible for the sales managers, while the executive leadership has the buck-stopping responsibility for this cascading accountability.

The CFO and her fellow executives could have made changes before they missed their sales numbers. They could have intervened with the senior sales leaders, who could then adjust with the sales managers, who could have helped their salespeople. My guess is that the leaders took their eyes off the ball and were embarrassed by missing what they promised the Street.

The upside of everything being your fault is that you are empowered to do something about any problem or challenge. If you are responsible for the results, you can make the changes necessary to remove any obstacles to revenue growth.

## Your Two Big Problems

Two problems prevent net new revenue: too few net new opportunities and two few won deals. No matter how busy you get or how many distractions jostle for your attention, these two problems must dominate your time and your energy. The reason you need several leadership styles, in fact, is so you can solve those problems more effectively.

### *Opportunity Creation: New Deals*

Let's return to the revenue growth formula:

$$\text{Existing Revenue} - \text{Churn} + \text{Net New Revenue}$$

The revenue that comes from your existing clients will not prevent you from increasing sales. It's just your starting number. While you may minimize churn, most organizations experience loss every year, and relegating your sales force to a client success role will remove them from their sales role. That leaves you with the one area you need to address: net new revenue.

The first problem is creating too few quality opportunities. Because you can never win an opportunity you didn't first create, creating new opportunities is critical to growth. However, most sales managers and sales leaders focus on capturing opportunities, often suffering from the delusion that they have plenty of opportunities in their pipeline.

The reason we covered both the external and internal factors that impact sales growth is because ignoring reality is a terrible strategy. Reality isn't concerned with your goals, your preferences, or your opinions. When buyers struggle to decide to change, the opportunities in your pipeline stall and die, even though you allow them to take up space and provide you and your team with false hope.

The reason many sales organizations miss their goals is because they believe they have more than enough opportunities to hit their aggressive targets. But when it becomes clear that many opportunities will not cross the line, sales managers push to make deals by discounting their price, even though price has little to do with the client's refusal to sign a contract, while also removing revenue—the very thing they need the most.

If you take only one thing from this book, make it this: charge your team to create more quality opportunities than you believe are necessary, since that is the only hedge available to you. In terms of leadership styles, this means you will need to become a transformational leader first, especially if your sales force doesn't prioritize prospecting. It's also likely you will have to take the role of autocrat, at least until your team caves in and recognizes that you won't permit them to wait you out.

## Opportunity Capture: Won Deals

I am first and foremost a salesperson. After that, I am a sales leader. I have spent equal time in both roles, working in a highly competitive industry where winning a client meant removing my competitor and taking their place.

My first four books codify what I believe to be a modern sales approach, one that addresses both the external and internal challenges of selling in today's environment. All four books were written to improve the sales force's effectiveness in the sales conversation, because it is the only vehicle available for winning deals. It does you no good to spend the time and energy creating new opportunities if you lose them—especially if your sales force lacks the effectiveness to create enough value for the client to prefer to buy from them.

Right now, the biggest obstacle to winning opportunities is that most sales organizations are still using legacy approaches to sales. There are still salespeople being taught and trained on strategies designed more than a half-century ago, for a very different environment. Many more are still using strategies and tactics closing in on the big 4-0—and equally ill-equipped for today's buyers, who need a different quality and quantity of help.

Salespeople offer their clients no value when they try to create credibility by talking up their company or their inspiring CEO, listing their existing clients and their testimonials, reciting their product brochures from memory, and finally asking a perfunctory question about the client's "problem." This pattern is the reason clients can't differentiate one salesperson (and their product) from the next, unless perhaps their logos are different colors.

Winning deals now requires helping clients recognize the forces that impact their business and their results. Modern salespeople must help their prospective clients discover something about themselves, creating a paradigm shift that causes the client to recognize new potential. This approach addresses the uncertainty that prevents clients from buying. Along similar lines, because buyers, decision-makers, and stakeholders need more—and different—help than they did in the past, it's necessary for the salesperson to facilitate a needs-based buyer's journey, exercising control over the process. One part of that journey is almost certain to be building consensus within the client's company.

While it is difficult to enable these competencies, they are fundamental—and they're often not easy ones to learn. In this environment, if you are not getting better at sales effectiveness, you're getting worse. Most sales leaders are so busy leading their teams that they missed the inflection point, one that gradually revealed that the world has changed, and selling and buying along with it.

Instead, most sales organizations are spending time and money on software, even though technology is far better at creating problems than solving them. You would be far better off training your sales force to be more effective in the one area that leads to revenue growth: their effectiveness in the conversations they have with decision-makers and the other stakeholders engaged in your sales conversation and their buying conversation. No one will decide to buy from you because of your sales tech stack, but they will buy from you if you provide the most help understanding how and why they need to change.

## A Focus on Revenue Growth

The ability to lead growth starts by understanding that your leadership is the first and most important variable to revenue growth. You will need to be a different leader if you want your team to do the work necessary for growth. To focus on net new revenue, you must lead your team to create and win the opportunities that will deliver your goal.

There are dozens of distractions that will confront you while you work on net new revenue, including new initiatives, tasks your company needs you to complete, and the daily problems and challenges that multiply every time someone darkens your door (or your inbox) with a problem they believe deserves your attention. To really reach your goals, you need a system, and that's what this book will teach you—a comprehensive and cohesive approach to revenue growth.

# 5

## Decision-Making

It's NOT UNCOMMON for a leader to acquire the unhealthy habit of avoiding decisions, especially difficult ones. A worse habit is dodging a decision because it requires one or more difficult conversations. But any serious effort to grow your revenue forces you to rectify problems, address challenges, and remove obstacles that prevent revenue growth—and the timing of these decisions is critical.

*Once you make a decision, immediately take action.*

This chapter will explore some of the decisions you'll need to confront, as well as some strategies to improve the effectiveness and efficiency of your decisions—even if you occasionally make mistakes.

## Prioritizing Big Problems

Most sales leaders are comfortable handling day-to-day, routine problems with their business, like when a prospective client pressures one of your salespeople for a discounted price, or when you provide a salesperson with strong direction on how to move a deal forward. Let's call these transactional decisions. While troubleshooting deals and giving advice often makes you feel productive and important, it also lets you avoid dealing with the larger, more difficult decisions you must make.

To grow your revenue, you must prioritize strategic decisions over transactional decisions. Here's a simple test to tell them apart: Will avoiding this decision have a negative impact on your ability to consistently increase your revenue? If so, it's most likely a strategic decision—especially if leaving it unaddressed will cause more harm over time. You've probably already heard the advice to act on your decisions as soon as you make them, but let me add a corollary: address and make decisions about issues that will harm your ability to grow revenue as soon as you recognize them. Here are a couple strategic decision scenarios that may sound familiar:

Two of your senior salespeople decided long ago that they were no longer going to prospect, even though they could create more value for a prospect than their less experienced teammates. In fact, it's been years since they created new opportunities or captured new logos. Because they've been allowed to avoid prospecting, you now must decide what to do with them, a choice that will directly impact your revenue.

Or how about this one? Your sales enablement team is still teaching and training your sales force in a legacy approach, telling them to spend the first 20 minutes of the sales call showing their prospective client pictures of your building, your existing clients' logos, and your product or services, all to set up the perfectly predictable question, "What's keeping you up at night?" Human resources won't let you change the training, but their sales approach is killing would-be deals at first contact with a decision-maker, costing you the revenue you need to hit your targets.

The reason people clean their desk (or their whole house) is often to feel productive while they're avoiding a more difficult task. You can always find something to busy yourself with, instead of dispatching the dragons that kill revenue. Avoiding hard decisions not only slows down your progress but also adds psychological weight to your day, making the already stressful work of leading growth even more challenging. Over time, even a relatively simple strategic decision can become overwhelming.

When you find yourself facing a strategic decision, it helps to make a plan. Determine the date by which you will take a decision, give yourself time to deliberate, and make a decision, even if you could potentially be wrong. Then take action.

## Decision Dates

Personally, I prefer to tackle my most difficult challenge first every day. The more difficult the conversation, the sooner I want to get it out of my way. Sometimes that can be done quickly, but many decisions require time to deliberate, as well as conversations with other people who may need to give feedback or at least be informed before you act on your decision. Often these conversations give you perspectives you hadn't considered or even alternative solutions you could try.

To avoid celebrating four birthdays (and dusting your desk way too often) while you struggle with a decision, start the process by determining a date by which you must decide. I'd budget a baseline of two weeks for complex strategic decisions, especially if you are going to seek the input of others. Scenario one, about the two senior salespeople, would fit in that category. But dealing with your legacy approach enablement team will probably require multiple conversations with senior leadership. This process may take months, but you can still give yourself a deadline for each conversation with a potential date for a decision.

## Deliberation Dates

Before you reach your decision date, you need to schedule time to deliberate—but not for so long you allow small monsters to grow into larger monsters. Problems don't age well. You will do some deliberating on your own, and some with people on your team or your own leaders. Here are some good ways to structure your deliberation.

Start your deliberation by writing down how the problem, challenge, obstacle, or individual harming your results. What does it cost you to continue to avoid taking action? The reason you need to make a difficult decision is so you can move forward and improve your results.

Many people avoid deciding because they fear negative consequences should they choose poorly, as well as the conflict they are sure to encounter when addressing a problem. We will have more to say about bad decisions and mistakes later, but when it comes to issues that harm your results, inaction is often the worst mistake you can make. Instead of letting lesser fears derail your decision, you must actively choose to address the greater danger. You should fear failing to meet your goals more than having a difficult conversation or making an unpopular choice. Those who allow the lesser fear to dominate their decisions will find leading growth more difficult than it should be.

Doing nothing is rarely the right choice, because you must continue to live with a problem that is harming your results. Take time to draft out the different choices available to you, including the ones that make you uncomfortable. Determine ahead of time if each choice is likely to provide the outcome you need. Any choice that fails that test should be taken off the table.

## Decide and Take Action

You have to make a decision about the two senior salespeople who are not contributing to growth. You also have to decide what to do about the enablement team that believes that 40-year-old sales strategies are still effective in the current environment. Leaving these difficult decisions unaddressed just so you can avoid difficult conversations and conflict with others will threaten your ability to achieve revenue growth.

The story that begins this book—the one in the prologue about the soldier who finally stepped forward and accepted the dangerous challenge to fight his drill sergeant—is there to remind you that you have to deal directly with your problems, challenges, and obstacles, even if it is unpleasant. As the leader, you are responsible for making the tough decisions.

Decision-making is like a muscle: the more you exercise it, the easier it becomes. Over time, your results will improve because you don't allow problems to persist. You might see other leaders stand by and allow their problems to continue, pretending they don't see them or that they aren't that serious. However, these indecisive leaders have tacitly lowered their standards, accepting a standard that is too low for their team to reach its full potential.

## You Will Make Mistakes

There is not always a way to ensure you make the best decision, even when you do the work. Sometimes your decision-making math is flawed, and the result is the opposite of what you expected. You must live with both your bad decisions and your good ones. The fact that you may not always make the right decision cannot prevent you from acting, especially when it's difficult.

When you make the right call and things work out as you believed they would, you can be proud of your decision. When you make the wrong call, you can be pleased that you decided and acquired the negative outcomes—feedback that gives you a data point that may improve the next decision with a similar fact pattern.

Once I heard a leader lament, "If it wasn't for employees and clients, I'd have no problems." You share this planet with seven billion, eight hundred million people. But you don't share their beliefs, their experiences, and their knowledge. You don't want to make "people" your problem. Instead, you want to start by separating the problem from the person, then try helping the person solve the problem. But when a person's behavior creates a problem, you must address their behavior and ensure they make the necessary change. We'll cover this in Chapter 9, a chapter on people.

There are a handful of revenue killers in every sales organization. Much of the time you have to help an individual change their beliefs, their commitment, and their behaviors. Very few people find it easy to change these things, often prompting a challenging but necessary decision. That takes us back to our prospecting problem, so let's look at it more closely.

## The Problem with Prospecting Problems

The problem with prospecting problems is that you need net new opportunities to create net new revenue. With too few opportunities you won't have enough coverage to ensure you reach your goals. Many sales leaders avoid making their sales force prospect, even when they know it's necessary, fearing that their sales force will think they are micromanaging them. The truth is that they are macromanaging the creation of new opportunities, one of the two major outcomes a salesperson needs to create. The pursuit of growth requires new opportunities.

As we mentioned earlier, imagine you have a couple of senior salespeople who have built a nice business with a couple large clients. Because they have held these clients for many years, they are comfortable with the money they earn, treating it like an annuity. Their role is closer to an account manager than an account executive.

Let's assume these salespeople are on a team of eight sales reps, which means that 25 percent (two out of eight) of that sales force creates no new clients. Those two reps won't add any new logos to your pipeline, making it difficult for the rest of the sales team to provide their portion of growth. You must do something about these two salespeople if you want revenue growth. There are several approaches you might consider.

First, because these salespeople are super-competent, you can require them to prospect for 90 minutes each day, with the expectation that they will schedule meetings. Because they handle large clients, you know they'll be excellent in front of new prospective clients.

Second, you could turn them into account managers, since that is the role they have chosen for themselves when they stopped prospecting. They might have to take a pay cut, but they may be happy anyway, giving you the opportunity to replace them with salespeople who are more than happy to prospect and win new deals.

The third possibility is to remove them or let them quit, something many sales leaders fear when a salesperson has managed a big client for years. But don't worry. You will have no trouble replacing them when you give the account to another salesperson, perhaps as a reward for winning a large client and a promise they will continue to prospect.

You may not have liked the idea of forcing your senior salespeople to prospect until you read the second choice (demote them to account managers) or the third choice (let them go). You can keep your two non-prospecting salespeople or you can grow your revenue, but you can't do both. More to the point, avoiding a decision teaches other salespeople to build a nice little client portfolio so they too can coast.

## The Right Opportunities

Let's look at another strategic decision. There are prospective clients that are right in your company's wheelhouse, your Dream Clients. They spend enough on what you sell to make them valuable to you, while also allowing you to create massive, strategic value for them. Some are giants, while others are medium-sized but profitable and capable of helping you reach your revenue goals. The remaining prospective clients are small, don't spend a lot in your category, and don't find what you do to be particularly strategic, even though they do need to buy what you sell.

But here's the rub: some percentage of your sales force believes that a deal is a deal, no matter how small, and no matter how unprofitable. Because they know larger clients already have a dance partner, they believe that other prospective clients will be easier to win—even if they are not a good fit for your revenue goals.

Your sales force is responsible for winning the clients your company needs, not the prospects they are comfortable calling on. Permitting individual salespeople to determine which opportunities to pursue and which to eschew can put your revenue growth at risk. When a client is too small, isn't the right fit, or is not worth the effort, throw it back and let some other company win their business. Some deals just won't generate enough revenue for the time and effort it takes to win them.

Your first option here is to flat-out eliminate the opportunities that are not right. You don't want to say no to opportunities, but when they are wrong for you, you must eliminate them from your pipeline. Your second choice might include asking the salespeople who want easy meetings to create a list of clients that are worth their time and energy. Your third choice may be to provide coaching, training, or development opportunities to help those salespeople succeed.

It's important to have the right opportunities, the ones that will allow you to generate net new revenue in excess of your churn. You must decide how to ensure you have the deals you need.

## Bad Attitudes and the Risk to Your Culture

While you may be the sales leader, there is often a person who acts as the "Sales Spiritual Leader," for lack of a better term. The sales force often looks to this person to know what is good and right and true. Occasionally, that person will support you, but more often they'll oppose your vision and put your culture at risk.

One Sales Spiritual Leader I encountered regularly told the sales force why their senior leader was wrong, why they didn't have to prospect and should wait for unsolicited RFPs, and why the company's high-trust, high-caring, and high-value approach was the reason they lost deals. This person's opinion was that the higher price was the real reason they lost. Because he was a strong personality and believed he was the smartest person in the room, he cowed others into supporting him—and the more people he won to his side, the more they tried to pressure their leader to change the company's model. He soon ruined the sales force and the culture.

The salesperson kept his job longer than I would have allowed, but I place a strong culture above any one person, especially when that person is infecting others with their poor beliefs. It can be difficult to remove a bad actor, but not half so difficult as rebuilding your entire sales culture into one that creates revenue growth and does good work. The longer you avoid making a decision that will prevent further damage, the worse your results.

In this case, you can start the process of removing the individual by collaborating with your human resources department, even though you may have to live through a few months of meetings and a lot of paperwork. Second, you can address them in front of your team every time they open their mouth to try to undermine you, explaining why what they say is incorrect and why they are really failing in sales. Third, you can require the person to attend coaching meetings twice a week and write a plan to improve their attitude, telling them you will decide if it's good enough. Once you reject a couple drafts and rewrite a couple more, you may find that they move on of their own accord.

What you cannot do is allow this person to ruin your sales force or undermine your leadership. When I was 12 years old, a 15-year-old kid punched me in the face. I didn't want to fight, but I had to fight to protect myself anyway. You may not want this conflict, but once it begins, you must end it. The upside of this is that people will know that you care about your team and your culture—and that you will defend it.

## "My Sales Style"

When a salesperson says they have their own style, what they mean is that they don't have an effective approach—and that they're smarter than you, your sales leadership team, and anyone else who cares about sales effectiveness. This "style" may include not prospecting effectively, poor planning, poor discovery, and generally winging it on meetings with what might have been a winnable client.

There is plenty of room for people to be creative within the sales conversation without rejecting your sales approach, your direction, your strategy, or anything else that you expect from your team. But there has to be a line. I recently saw a salesperson who created their own sequences instead of using the one their company created. The emails had almost no text at all, instead providing links to a blog post. While his intentions were good, his strategy was weaker than circus lemonade.

It can be difficult for a person who is doing something they're comfortable with to understand why they are failing and why others are successful. But when you install a sales approach, you do so because you believe it is the best way to create and win deals. It isn't something you offer up as a possible choice in a buffet of sales approaches. Instead, it's your way of making certain your team creates compelling, differentiated value, the kind that results in won deals and a high level of effectiveness in the sales conversation.

Effectiveness is part of the revenue growth formula. It doesn't make sense to work hard at growing revenue if your work doesn't produce results. Your first choice when making this decision is to require the style-happy salesperson to retrain on the correct approach and to demonstrate it in the field, preferably with you observing and encouraging them to keep working on their technique. Second, you can require coaching and role-playing in a safe environment, as you are trying to help the salesperson succeed. Finally, if the person isn't willing to practice the approach you require, they will have to move on to find a company that believes their "style" will work for them.

As we've seen before, when you leave strategic problems, challenges, and obstacles unaddressed, they will harm your results. Don't wait to make decisions.

## Decisions About Your Work

One of the ways I check my decision-making is by keeping a decision journal. By writing down the decisions you make, what you believed would happen before making the decision, and how it turned out in the end, you'll get better at making decisions. You will also be looking at the decision more objectively, making it easier for you to make good decisions fast.

We cannot leave this chapter without turning the spotlight on the decisions you make about the everyday work you do. Each time you clock in, you have a choice to make: Will you help your team succeed or just find busywork to keep the folks upstairs happy with you? You cannot serve two masters without disappointing one or both, so it's important to decide whom you are going to disappoint and how you intend to do so. And your company already has more than enough sycophants, so the most reliable way to advance in your career is by ensuring your team meets their goals.

There are a lot of things that you might do with your time, but if a task doesn't have you working with your team, you are putting revenue growth at risk. Sure, you could volunteer to spearhead the Task Force for Revamping the CRM Dashboard Interface (TFRCDI for short), but that's like leaving the sidelines to go change the lights on the scoreboard. You're the coach, and that means confidently knowing your place. Besides, there is nothing inside your company that will generate new revenue; all the revenue you need is found outside of your four walls.

Sales leaders often complain that they don't have enough time to do their work, and there is little doubt the role of sales manager is difficult. But still, you have the very same number of hours in a day as everyone else on this planet. There is plenty of time for what you believe is most important, as long as you avoid wasting time on things that cannot move the needle toward greater revenue.

More concretely, the more time you spend working with your team, the better their results will be. If you avoid that simple act, inevitably some significant percentage of your sales force will be struggling, confused, and disengaged. Giving time to your team will improve their results, while giving time to your internal obligations will contribute nothing to your results. For instance, some research suggests that salespeople want more coaching from their sales managers. They want personal and professional development and more help with deal strategy. In short, they want to grow, develop, and improve their results. Maybe you don't think there's time to coach every individual on your team. But the less you live in your inbox, the more time you'll have for the people you are counting on to produce the results you need. Internally, aim for minimum viable compliance. Externally, aim for maximum engagement and the better results that accrue to a well-trained, well-coached, and well-developed team of salespeople.

# 6

# Strategy and Alignment

THE NEW SALESPERSON you hired isn't selling the way you believe they should. At their last job, they were taught to win deals by promising a lower price than whatever their prospective client was paying. You are unhappy that the salesperson keeps asking you to support this concession, not just because it's unnecessary but because it reduces both your revenue and the profit you should be capturing for improving the client's results.

If you want your team to succeed in creating and winning new opportunities, you need to provide them with an appropriate strategy and align all your efforts to that strategy. Your strategy provides guidance on how you compete for and win opportunities—and new logos. No matter what strategy you pursue, it is best to be a purist, never deviating from your choice and requiring your team to use the same strategy in all situations.

Most sales leaders explain how they intend to compete and win by sharing the name of their sales approach: "Solutions Selling," "Challenger," "Strategic Selling," "Consultative Selling," "Needs-Satisfaction Selling," and so on. But these are approaches, not strategies. (These approaches are more branding than substance.) Put another way, they'd all qualify as separate species under the genus "Consultative Sales Approaches." In that model, my own approach would be Genus: Consultative Sales; Species: Level 4 Value Creation™. There are many solid approaches in that genus, but you shouldn't confuse them with your sales strategy.

## The Two Major Sales Strategies

Understanding your strategy and ensuring your team is executing it effectively are both central to revenue growth. When rogue salespeople want to make sales easier, they stray away from your strategy and create problems that harm your results, including breaking your company's delivery model by not capturing enough of the value you create (i.e., profit) to be able to provide the better results the client needs. Your sales strategy must match your company's model for your team—and your company—to succeed and grow.

There are two major strategies a sales force might execute to find success. Let's call the first option a transactional strategy. A transactional approach is designed to provide your client with something they need, without any friction or complications. Most sales managers and salespeople who haven't experienced transactional selling find it difficult, because there is very little conversation or consultation. It's mostly a straight pitch to buy what you sell. Consultative salespeople might even poke fun at transactional sellers for being order-takers, even though that is exactly what their strategy is designed to enable.

The second major option is a consultative strategy. The word *consultative* means you provide business advice, telling someone what they need to do to improve their results. Most salespeople mistakenly believe that consultative sales means they don't use any high-pressure tactics and ask their prospects a series of questions, mostly questions designed to elicit a problem. A truly consultative strategy is built on counsel, advice, and recommendations. Many of the approaches under the consultative strategy form some version of "Solution Selling," which we'll come back to later.

## Transactional Strategy

The transactional strategy works well when your prospective client needs to buy something they buy frequently and where there is not a great chance of the product or service failing. If there is a problem, the negative consequences aren't likely to harm the client, because they can easily buy a new one from another salesperson at a different company. However, there are exceptions where a transactional failure can cause serious harm, like a construction crew whose materials never showed up, costing their company time and money even though the crew was on site and ready to work.

Here is another example of a transactional strategy. Imagine you sell a small, cheap computer chip. Your inside sales team calls small manufacturers to ask them to buy your computer chips. Because they are so cheap, it's easy for the buyer to place an order. Because there is little risk, your strategy is built on asking people directly to buy your chips, something they buy all the time. A transactional strategy is designed to transact, removing any complexity or friction from the purchase process.

The internet was supposed to eliminate transactional salespeople by selling anything and everything that can be sold, without needing a dedicated salesperson. While the internet has eliminated some salespeople who used a transactional strategy, there are still very large sales organizations that use this strategy to earn billions of dollars in revenue each year.

## Consultative Strategy

The second major strategy is consultative, and it is everything that the transactional strategy is not. The consultative strategy is useful when your clients need counsel, advice, and recommendations so they can make the right decision for their company and their future results. Much of the time, the decision could have serious negative consequences if the client makes the wrong call.

To avoid these consequences, the consultative strategy is designed to help the client make the right decision by providing them good counsel, helping the decision-makers use what they buy to produce the desired outcome, and avoiding mistakes that might disrupt their business. In general, a consultative strategy works best when the client rarely makes this decision and when it is strategic enough that they must get it right.

While advice has always played some role in sales, modern buyers and decision-makers need more from salespeople, including greater insights, more help guiding their buyer's journey, and more expertise as they manage their change initiative. What once was "consultative enough" is increasingly inadequate.

## Both Strategies, Two Sales Forces

Let's stick with our chip-maker scenario. There are companies whose inside and outside sales teams both call on clients but using different strategies. The inside team uses a transactional strategy, calling their clients to acquire orders, a strategy that helps their clients by making sure they have what they need. The outside team works with gargantuan companies that buy millions of these chips every quarter, requiring a consultative approach, since the purchase is strategic and the large clients' needs and expectations are much greater than the small manufacturers. The outside team's consultative strategy helps solve the challenges of the large manufacturer who struggles, for example, with service-level agreements.

Sales leaders sometimes choose the wrong strategy, ruining their sales force and failing to grow their revenue. But where sales organizations really get in trouble is allowing salespeople to practice a strategy that doesn't match their goals.

### How to Ruin a Sales Force with the Wrong Strategy

One company I am familiar with had excellent service, great financial backing, and all the pieces in place to grow their revenue. Their senior sales leader, however, believed the transactional strategy was the fastest way to acquire new clients and new revenue. Because that leader imposed a transactional strategy, the sales force was limited to a single sales call, the legendary "one-call close."

Unfortunately, the company's prospects rejected that strategy: many prospective clients weren't prepared to sign a contract at the end of the call, even though it required no money upfront. The service they provided also created a conflict with the prospective clients' business model, frightening many of their prospects away. Even though their clients would have improved their results and increased their overall profitability, they rejected the offer, and many who signed a contract never executed the company's service. In fact, the salespeople who ignored the demand to close in one call were winning clients and helping those clients succeed, even if the sales force had to fudge their reports by leaving off the additional meetings.

Eventually, the company lost many salespeople who could successfully execute a consultative strategy, taking their time and teaching their prospective client why they should change, how they should change, and how to build consensus within their teams. The mismatch between the senior leader's required strategy and what was working for clients ruined the sales force and harmed the company's overall results.

## Market Leaders and Their Disciplines

In their wonderful book titled *The Discipline of Market Leaders*, Fred Wiersema and Michael Treacy provide three major strategies from market leaders. Even though there are three different models, the companies that employ them are purists, never straying from who and what they are. Understanding these three strategies will help you determine which strategy is closest to the one you need to achieve lift.

The first strategy is to always have the lowest price. As sales leaders and salespeople, we believe that stressing a low price makes selling easy, and it is true that you can sell more by taking price out of the equation. But as it pertains to execution, having the lowest price is the most difficult of the three strategies. You must gain concessions from your suppliers and your employees, passing off the savings to your clients. Salespeople who want to provide concessions don't know that those concessions don't fit in your strategy or your delivery model (i.e., the value you create). Low-price strategies are transactional, not consultative.

The second strategy is to always have the best product. There are computer companies, car companies, hotels, restaurants, and jewelry shops that provide luxuries above and beyond their competition. While you might have a great product or service, you may not be at the level of the companies that continually reimagine and recreate their products or services, always raising the bar. You know this is your strategy when you release a new product to great fanfare and a line of clients stretching around the block. Maintaining that pace requires enough profit to continually innovate. These companies don't provide discounts because it breaks their delivery model.

The third and final strategy is one Wiersema and Treacy call "Customer Intimacy." Many, if not most, consultative strategies are really executing this strategy. It's built on providing your client with the best solution, solving their problems, building custom solutions that will work for individual clients, and having product expertise. This model will find you competing against lookalike competitors, some who will have a delivery model that allows for a lower price, confusing salespeople and causing them to wonder why their company can't discount their prices. Of the three strategies, this one requires the most sales effectiveness, because you cannot point to your lower prices or your best-in-class product or service, so you need to sell effectively. We'll come back to sales effectiveness in Chapter 10.

The terms *transactional* and *consultative* don't provide enough clarity to help salespeople understand how they are supposed to compete and win, and why they can't do some of the things that other companies do routinely. As a leader, you need to be able to teach your team what is good and right and true. You also need to help them understand your choice of strategy.

## A List of Substrategies

There are a number of different substrategies operating in the major categories of transactional and consultative strategies. Different companies execute them at different times to reach their goals, including revenue growth. Not all these strategies are right for every sales organization, but all are worth knowing, because they allow you to create initiatives that lead to revenue growth.

### Predatory Pricing

My introduction to predatory pricing came when a client told me (by letter) that he had removed me and my company and replaced us with a competitor that had just moved into my city. Up until that point, all the companies in my industry had very nice margins, and there was enough business for everyone based on their appetite for growth. To acquire the revenue and profit they needed to support their operations, this new predator lowered their pricing enough that it created an irresistible offer for companies that were spending millions of dollars annually. My company and all our competitors lost clients to the new shark in the Red Ocean, greeting us by stealing our clients.

To compete with our terrible new neighbor, other companies started to lower their prices, not knowing that the predatory pricing was only being used to capture enough clients to be able to operate in the market. A lot of salespeople don't pay attention to business, so they weren't aware that Toyota had used this very strategy to enter U.S. auto markets. Like Toyota, however, the predator had no interest in giving their new clients the same pricing in the future—the whole point of predatory pricing is to establish yourself in a market, then raise your prices later. As more companies entered our industry, the prices never went back to where they were before.

## The Land Grab

You could use predatory pricing as part of a land grab, but the main goal in a land grab is to beat your competitors to a market and capture the clients there, so you can prevent the competition from making those acquisitions. Winning clients first becomes especially important when the switching costs are high or when there is little meaningful difference between you and your competitors.

The transactional senior leader I mentioned earlier really needed a land grab, a strategy that would have worked if the sales force had been allowed to execute a basic consultative strategy. You want to capture the clients, even if it takes time, as trying to speed up the buying process and losing means you may let your competition capture that client.

## Competitive Displacement

You may have heard of the Blue Ocean Strategy by W. Chan Kim and Renée Mauborgne, both professors at INSEAD. A Blue Ocean Strategy is one that provides you with a competitive advantage. The opposite of a Blue Ocean is a Red Ocean, a result of the blood-stained waters caused by the ferocious predators fighting over clients.

Many sales organizations must displace their competition to win a client's business. My book *Eat Their Lunch: Winning Customers Away from Your Competition* describes how to do just that. The company that executed the predatory pricing treated each sale as if it were a transaction, but most competitive displacements require a consultative approach, one that compels the client to change.

There are a dozen reasons your prospective client might shuffle your competitor out and move their business to you, including complacency, a sense of entitlement, apathy, a resentment they can feel, and the introduction of new stakeholders. But the one that seems best suited to allow a displacement is a systemic challenge that your competitor has left unaddressed, the equivalent of locking the windows but leaving the front door wide open.

The strategy for a displacement starts with capturing mindshare: explain to the client what's going on, how their environment has changed, and how these trends will harm their business—if it isn't doing so already. Think of it this way: your prospective client now needs something better. Displacement requires a patient, professional persistence over time.

I grew up in the Red Ocean, and I know it well. When you live in that environment, you don't want to be a clownfish, no matter who finds you. You want to be an orca, the only animal that preys on great white sharks.

## Champion-Challenger

The champion-challenger strategy is a derivative of a competitive displacement by capturing some—but not all—of the client's spending in your area. This strategy leaves the client's existing supplier in place (even though they are going to be unhappy to share their client with you) but takes some part of the business away from them, forcing the champion to work harder to keep their existing position while you challenge them by acquiring what used to be their orders, eventually siphoning off significant revenue.

The goal in the champion-challenger strategy is eventually to take the lion's share of the business by being more attentive, more engaged, and performing better than the champion. Executing this strategy can help you become the champion, demoting your competitor to the role of challenger. All you need to execute this strategy is a client who is not getting what they need from their existing supplier, as no decision-maker is going to lose their clients to protect a vendor (that's how they get displaced).

## Land and Expand

When you offer several products or services, the land-and-expand strategy is an excellent way to build revenue: you start by winning one piece of business, then leverage the opportunity to introduce additional products or services. Companies with many ways to create value for the client can continue to create that new value by adding to what they are already doing.

Another way to execute this strategy is to acquire new departments, divisions, and subsidiaries by asking your contacts to testify on your behalf and introduce you to their contacts. Most sales organizations suggest that they want to land and expand, but it's much easier to expand sales at your first "landing" site than to expand to new ones. Even within the same client company, most other departments already have partners in place, don't know their peers well enough to entertain their recommendation, or just don't want to go through the pain of changing.

## Channel Partners

Quite a few companies employ channel partners to sell on their behalf, especially in tech industries where companies sell a wide range of products and services to their clients. When you look at a company like CDW, you'll find products from multiple companies, many of them competing for the same client's business.

This strategy is a way to control the cost of sales while gaining access to the channel partner's clients. The channel partner might employ a transactional strategy, a consultative strategy, or both.

## Alignment and Revenue Growth

As a growth leader, it is necessary to create alignment around your strategy, supporting it with an approach that allows your team to execute that strategy to create and win deals. If your strategy is consultative, everyone on your team will need to pursue consultative deals and use the approach you employ. No salesperson can be allowed to decide to sell using a transactional strategy or approach.

The same is true if your team needs a transactional strategy, something difficult for consultative salespeople who are used to creating value in the sales conversation. If you should be trans-acting, transact by calling and acquiring orders. When there is no greater value created through consultation, there is no reason to spend time trying to create value your client doesn't want or need. Most often, they just want to know your price and when you can deliver what they need.

You lose opportunities for net new revenue when salespeople don't understand the strategy (say, consultative), and the approach (modern insight-based approach) necessary to creating and winning opportunities. The salesperson who doesn't create any value for the client in a consultative strategy—often because they spend too much time talking about your company, your clients, and your solutions—isn't leveraging the insights, good counsel, advice, or recommendations that would prove they can provide better results.

## Imposing Your Strategy and Your Approach

Strategy is mostly made up of what you decide not to do. Southwest Airlines won't move your luggage or give you anything more than pretzels, the Ritz Carlton doesn't discount rooms, and the spammers who call you to sell you a new car warranty never take you off their list.

A telltale sign that a company doesn't have a strategy is that they don't refuse prospective clients or deals that are not right for their business. Your strategy requires you to refuse what is not right for your business, imposing standards that don't permit salespeople to waste time on what you know you don't want.

In one of my businesses, we have no interest in small clients. Instead, we pursue large clients with equally large needs, who also believe what we do is a strategic part of their business. That makes what we sell important enough to be worth investing their time and a little higher price than many of our competitors. We refuse small users because they take time and resources away from what we really want.

One leader asked me, "How do you say no to a deal a salesperson brings to you?" You say, "No. We don't want that." By lowering your standards and accepting anything, you are permitting the salesperson to avoid the strategy. You will get a lot more of anything you accept, even if it's not what you need.

It is the sales leader's responsibility to impose a strategy and an approach that ensures their team wins the deals necessary to create revenue growth. The imposition of a strategy ensures that you don't break your company's delivery model by pursuing deals that are not the right fit. To do this, you must teach, train, and defend your strategy and your approach.

## Organizational Alignment

You also need to align your strategy and your approach with your company's overall strategy for delivering value. There is no reason to exert the effort to acquire clients that are not right for your company, even though a lot of sales organizations do just that—then struggle to help the client or their company. Depending on the size of your company, you may also need to gain alignment with your senior leadership team, ensuring they support your strategy.

Most of all, you must spend the time and energy aligning your sales force behind the strategy, your approach, and the clients you want. The salesperson who tells you they have their own "style" will learn a new one. The salesperson who is used to working for someone who will say yes to every deal will learn to accept a "hard no" when they bring you a deal that isn't close to meeting your standards. The person who is used to being able to run to their sales manager to negotiate a concession for their prospective client will learn to say no to the first ask, then to negotiate something you can accept—without negotiating with you.

You can save a lot of time, energy, and conversations by ensuring your strategy explains what you do, why you do it, how you do it, and all the things you don't want. Violating your strategy earns an automatic no, a blanket decision that isn't eligible for any appeal to you, the House of Representatives, the president of the United States, or even the judges on *The Voice*.

Strategy is worth the managerial will it requires to gain alignment, as it makes certain you are doing the right work, at the right time, with the right targets, in the right way. It also ensures your company can take care of the clients you acquire, something that must be true for those contracts to produce the net new revenue that results in growth.

# PART

# III

# Accountability, People, and Effectiveness

IN THIS SECTION, you are going to put several pieces in place that will ensure you reach your goals. First, we'll work on creating a positive culture of accountability, and then we'll add some structures you will put in place to make the change stick—without you having to nag and pester your sales team. With these pieces in place, we can turn our attention to what is most important: people! The last chapter in this section will provide you strong guidance on improving your team's effectiveness.

# 7

## Accountability

WHY DO SOME sales organizations produce growth year after year while similarly situated competitors wallow in stagnation, often for years on end? Both those that grow and those that stall have smart and motivated professionals leading their sales teams. Both offer products or services that clients need and buy. So, what makes the difference? In my experience, it comes down to one thing: accountability.

You already know that it's difficult to grow without a detailed vision of better results and a better future. That vision must be supported by accountability. But not just any accountability: consistent accountability built on a positive culture, one that expects everyone to do what is required of them and to keep their commitments. Do not mistake it for a negative culture, where leaders use threats, pressure, and other forms of coercive force to, *ahem*, motivate their sales force.

I once saw a new CEO chastise his sales leaders and his sales force, wasting an opportunity to create a positive culture. But he poisoned the room by criticizing both the sales force and their leaders, even cursing at them for poor results he believed were their fault. In a single afternoon, he created a negative culture and caused several leaders to look for a way out of the company. Soon after his tirade, the company's industry melted down, reducing their already meager revenue and increasing the leader's desperation. But by then the sales team knew where he stood, so when he needed them to move heaven and earth to regain lost revenue, they were unwilling even to try.

Coercive force is the choice of weak leaders, the kind who lack the emotional intelligence and persuasive skills to influence others. You often see it when leaders are self-oriented, believing their people should cater to the leader's needs instead of taking care of the people on the team. The autocrat is not capable of creating a positive culture of accountability, which is the surest path to sustainable growth.

## Balancing Autonomy and Discipline

Few professional roles come with as much autonomy as sales. Those with a strong will and self-discipline do well in roles that provide maximum freedom. However, there are others who lack the discipline to do what is required without resistance—even if they don't audibly object, they often avoid necessary work, especially necessary work they don't personally enjoy. Without enough self-discipline to temper the autonomy of sales roles, salespeople fail to do the right work at the right time in the right way.

My preference is to hire people with enough self-discipline to do their work without being told or reminded. I already have three children, and I am not interested in acquiring additional dependents at work. Besides, my primary leadership style is laissez-faire, making it difficult for me to live with a person who needs me to nudge them to do their work. A salesperson who can't take advantage of opportunities is too great a risk to revenue growth.

Fortunately, there are ways to provide discipline to your team, and accountability is one incredibly powerful strategy for producing revenue growth. In this chapter, you'll learn how to create a positive culture of accountability that supercharges your results.

## Psychological Safety and a Positive Culture

In *Smarter, Faster, Better: The Secret of Being Productive in Life and Business*, author Charles Duhigg recounts how Google, the search engine that has effectively replaced the term "search engine," did a study to discover what made great managers so effective. To their surprise, the deciding factor was less about the leader and more about how their teams operated: it was the norms established in the workplace. As Duhigg put it,

"Norms determine whether we feel safe or threatened, ener-vated or excited and motivated or discouraged by teammates." In another study, a scholar named Amy Edmondson was study-ing medical mistakes when she discovered that "it wasn't sim-ply that strong teams encouraged open communication and weak teams discouraged it.. . . In an interview, [a] nurse man-ager explained that a 'certain level of error will occur' so a 'nonpunitive environment' is essential to deal with this error productively."

This makes sense if you think about employees' needs. Maslow's model identifies a hierarchy of human needs, organ-ized as a pyramid. At the base are our physiological needs, fol-lowed by psychological safety and then belonging. When you threaten a person's job, like the CEO who created a nega-tive culture, you create uncertainty about the three founda-tional needs that make up the widest part of the pyramid. In Chapter 9, we'll go over a structure you can use when someone on your team is struggling to produce results, without having to resort to threats.

What the nurse manager called "a nonpunitive environment" is the core of psychological safety. Like nurses, salespeople often work long, stressful hours, and both groups often face poor treat-ment from colleagues and managers. They're going to make mis-takes. But in a positive culture of accountability, those mistakes are opportunities to improve, since every salesperson knows they have the support of their manager and team.

I learned this long before I ever read Duhigg's book. Having worked in staffing for decades, I noticed that companies that provided a positive environment not only had the best reten-tion rates but could often offer lower pay rates. I also saw what happens when a company treats employees as a means to an end. One person commented during an exit interview that, from an employee perspective, the company was "a cross between a daycare center and a maximum-security prison." Soon afterwards, candidates would refuse to work at the company before they were even offered a position. We tried to change the company's bad behavior, but a fish rots from the head, and the managers were the spitting image of their executive leaders.

We will return to psychological safety and the need for a positive culture later in this chapter. But now let's look at the components of accountability and strategies for incorporating them into your team.

## Raising Your Standards and Expectations

The CEO of my family business watched me walk into the office one day. There was a little scrap of paper on the lobby floor, and I had walked by it without picking it up. She stopped me and asked why I hadn't put the paper in the wastebasket. Her standards were higher than mine; she believed that our lobby was a representation of who we were as a company. Mainly to appease her, I retraced my steps, picked up the paper, and threw it away.

It would be some time before I discovered that "how you do one thing is how you do everything." Soon after that, I raised my standards and started demanding more of myself and my sales teams. Because you are pursuing a vision and a transformation, you are certain to need to raise your standards, especially around the activities and outcomes that lead to growth.

## Setting Your Expectations

You cannot hold someone accountable for something until they know what you expect from them. It is unfair to be unhappy with a person who doesn't meet your unspoken expectations, yet it is common for leaders to assume their team can read their mind when it comes to workplace standards.

Clarifying these expectations is critical to accountability, which means it is your responsibility to communicate what you want in a way that everyone understands. Leaving those expectations unspoken will prevent you from having a positive culture of accountability. Let's say you are frustrated because too many members of your sales team avoid prospecting. If all you do is "suggest" that your team might benefit from spending more time prospecting, you have not communicated your expectations. Setting an expectation would sound more like this: "I expect you to prospect for 90 minutes each day, and double that if you are unable to schedule three meetings each week." This is a clear and measurable expectation, one that doesn't need further explanation or a negotiation. One of my expectations is that my team is a "phone first" sales organization: we call prospective clients to schedule a meeting instead of emailing, because we prioritize effectiveness over efficiency.

Any time you are frustrated that some team members are not doing what they need to do to succeed, restate and reinforce your expectations and ensure that everyone understands them.

## *Delivering a Due Date*

Accountability requires something be done by a date and time. Without a deadline, there is no accountability, as the clock will just keep running.

In the example above, the deadline for the 90 minutes of prospecting (or 180 minutes, if the salesperson books fewer than three meetings a week) is the end of the day. The additional time is not punitive. How could it be when prospecting is one of the primary tasks of a salesperson? Instead, it helps the salesperson succeed by creating the opportunities they need.

As I mentioned in the introduction to this book, one of the external obstacles to creating new revenue is the time-bound nature of sales. We have quarterly and annual goals, and those goals require that the right work be done in the right way and at the right time. When your work isn't done on time, you miss your goals. When I sold in a service industry, for instance, it was important to win large deals going into the start of the year. The later in the year a deal was won, the less revenue we could generate from the client. Conversely, winning clients early in the year meant more revenue. Because clients paid weekly, winning a deal at the end of the year would produce no revenue, but at least I'd get 12 months in the next year.

At the end of every year, unfortunately, some large percent of salespeople disengage, telling themselves that no one wants to meet with them. That rapidly becomes a self-fulling prophecy, especially because no one meets with a salesperson who doesn't call to ask them for a meeting. As a result, the salesperson does too little prospecting in November and December, giving up four or five weeks. When January arrives, they convince themselves that their prospective clients are just getting back to work, so they give up a large part of January to "settle back in" to the work they should have been doing all along.

Let's assume your sales cycle is 90 days long. Missing opportunities from November means you are missing deals you would have closed in February. The missed opportunities from December become the missing deals you needed to win in March. No opportunities created in January means no captured opportunities in April. Because you can't cheat time or the sales cycle, you must do the work when it is due.

## Purpose and Meaning

When you require a person on your team to produce a result by a certain time, you must also clarify why it is important to achieve those results by the due date. Purpose and meaning improves your team's commitment to achieving the outcome.

There is nothing worse than being told to do something "because I said so"; to make a task feel like a punishment, make someone do something without helping them understand how it contributes to their success and to your overall mission and vision. By adding meaning and purpose, you make the task and its result something important—a contribution, not just a checkbox.

I know that many people like Simon Sinek's book *Start with Why*. Sinek believes that people buy from companies because of why they do what they do. My experience is that "who" is a stronger force than "why." "Who we are" may not make for a great sales pitch, but it is a more powerful motivation when it comes to accountability. Here is an example: "The reason we prioritize opportunity creation is because we are a growth company focused on winning clients that need our help improving their results—and we do it better than anyone." The focus on clients can help ensure your sales force is other-oriented, instead of the self-orientation that leads to bad sales conversations.

It's your responsibility to explain why what you do is important if you want people to be accountable for their results.

## Providing Resources

Because individuals on your team are likely better at some sales skills than others, they may need additional help to produce the result you expect of them. If you have resources that would improve their results, make sure your team knows what they can do to get help. That will improve their ability to deliver results as well as their trust in your leadership. Your team should know what to do if they need help, whom to talk to, and what resources are available to help them. Much like you help your clients change before they fail, a positive culture of accountability requires you to intervene before an individual salesperson fails to meet an important commitment.

Whether that intervention involves training, coaching, working with a more experienced salesperson, or role-playing with well-designed scripts, providing individuals with the help they need improves their ability to be accountable for the result you both need to grow revenue. Later, we'll look at strategies to develop your sales team's competencies.

## The Heart of Accountability

One of the reasons sales organizations don't have the accountability they need is because they believe their work is done when they set their expectations. But the heart of accountability isn't asking someone to commit to achieving an important result. In fact, there is no accountability without reviewing those results—or the lack thereof.

Whenever you set an expectation for your team or an individual, you must also schedule a time when you can take account of the results. Skipping these accountability meetings tells your team that you are not serious about your expectations. If for some reason you can't meet at the scheduled time, reschedule it for your first available slot, even if it's 7 a.m. on Monday. The meeting to capture the results is every bit as important as the one to set expectations, since by definition accountability requires attention to results.

Later, I'll share some strategies for accountability meetings that will help ensure your team produces the right results, even when a few of your more challenging salespeople do their best to wait you out. While holdouts might hope and pray that all this accountability goes away, I have it on good authority that the Gods of Revenue Growth will have your back, so long as you never give up or give in.

## Humane Consequences

When your team members mess up, the consequences should always be humane. Imagine that your son or daughter just took a new job, one that makes them accountable for some important result. But they're having a tough time catching on, and after a few days their manager is not happy with their results. How would you want their manager to treat them? The people who struggle to meet your expectations are someone else's daughter or son or father or mother, and you should treat them like you would expect the people you care about to be treated.

The starting point for humane consequences is more training and coaching. You will find that some people need more time to learn, especially with something as complex as B2B sales. A few individuals will not do the work they need to do in the time they need to do it. In these cases, shortening the time between accountability meetings removes the ability for someone to wait you out. You don't have to be angry or punitive; adding more frequent reviews is often enough to cause a person to increase their effort and their activity. Accountability isn't punishment; it's a guardrail to protect your employee (and your company) from a much worse future outcome.

Training and coaching won't always be enough, but even then, you should not make consequences punitive. I recommend working through these three stages, almost always in this order:

1. **Retrain and coach the individual.** You hired the person, and you are responsible for helping them succeed. If you see progress, you may keep them in their current role. If not, at some point you must move to the next option.

2. **Reassign the individual to another role.** Selling isn't as easy as some people believe. Often, you find a good employee in a role for which they are poorly suited. A bad account executive is often a wonderful account manager, usually because they are uncomfortable prospecting. Helping someone pursue a role better suited to their skills is humane, and you never have to feel bad about helping them succeed.

3. **Remove the individual.** When you have exhausted your first two choices, you are left with removing the individual from your team. At this point they aren't likely to be surprised by your decision, and they may have already decided to move on.

There are two exceptions to this patient approach that we need to address. First, keeping a negative person—the kind who actively works against your goals and tries to recruit others to join them—is too great a risk to your positive culture. Negativity is the only cancer that spreads by contact; you cannot allow it to metastasize inside your team. Second, certain breaches of integrity would require you to remove the individual from your team and your company immediately. These include major infractions like the fraudulent padding of an expense report.

## Clean Hands and Intervention

The theory of clean hands suggests that you must do everything you can to help an individual succeed before you take any negative action. Your team is always watching how you treat people, whether those people are succeeding or struggling. They need to know that when they inevitably find themselves in a slump, they will be treated humanely and professionally, as a valued member of your team. This strategy creates psychological safety and a positive culture of accountability.

When you put forth the effort to help a salesperson improve their results, your team will know that you did everything in your power to help turn things around. In short, your actions will be seen as fair, even though the salesperson may find themselves in another role or working for another company. But before you ever get to that stage, work hard to prevent negative outcomes.

Before we leave this section, I must leave you with one critically important strategy for maintaining a positive culture of accountability. One mistake that sales managers routinely make is waiting for a salesperson to fail before they intervene. It's never good to let an individual fail, and the reason we build a positive culture of accountability is so we can intervene early, preventing that failure.

It's not fair to stand by and watch as a member of your team flounders. Leaders with a "sink or swim" mentality will always allow a member of their team to drown. A leader who believes in "sink or swim" would do well to provide swimming lessons before throwing a person in the deep end of the pool. Don't be fooled: even the strong swimmers on your team will watch and learn how and when you intervene. For your sake and theirs, intervene at the first sign of trouble. Pipeline meetings and other structures of accountability can serve as an early warning signal. The sooner you help a salesperson adjust, the greater their chances of succeeding.

## Establishing Your Nonnegotiables

By now you know you need not be an autocrat, a dictator, or Cersei Lannister. You can lead your team to growth without ruling with an iron fist. You are always better off building your approach on solid values and principles, then transferring them to your team. However, there is room to establish a few nonnegotiable outcomes, the kind your team cannot miss without making revenue growth more difficult—or even impossible.

Keep this list short, perhaps three to five items. Too many nonnegotiables will poison your culture and cause your team to disengage, especially if they feel that they have no voice and their ideas are ignored or rejected. The same thing happens when companies send out an engagement survey but make no changes after the results are tallied. The goal is enrollment and commitment, not compliance. You need buy-in for your few but critically important nonnegotiables.

## Identifying Your Nonnegotiables

Let's start by removing honesty and integrity. These values are so important that they should go without saying, so they don't count against your limit. Instead, start by identifying the most powerful activities and outcomes you believe are critical to growth. By now, I hope your list includes "opportunity creation" and "opportunity capture."

One sales organization I am familiar with mandated that every email must be returned within 24 hours. Given that an average employee receives 127 emails each day and sends close to 40, the math is just untenable. Assuming it takes 3 minutes to read and respond to an email, you will have committed your team to over 6 hours of email every day. Time spent returning email is time taken away from the few things that create revenue growth. This is not an appropriate nonnegotiable.

A more tenable requirement is for the whole sales team to do a 90-minute prospecting block each morning at 9 a.m., especially if their leader believes prospecting is central to her vision. Some on the team might start calling her Cersei behind her back, at least until they start doubling their meetings, opportunities, and commissions. This activity and the outcomes that naturally follow make it a perfect nonnegotiable. Your nonnegotiable doesn't necessarily have to entail making everyone prospect, but it won't hurt to devote an hour and a half each day to booking meetings and creating net new opportunities.

Whatever ends up on your list, pick practices that will contribute the most to your growth goals. You must defend each nonnegotiable without fail and without exception, even with your most successful and/or senior salespeople. And by the way, there is no reason to allow your best salespeople to avoid prospecting. They have the most experience and the greatest ability to create value for your prospective clients. Too many sales organizations miss their revenue goals because they don't insist their best sales reps prospect. Even worse, those exceptions let the rest of the sales force look forward to a time when they no longer need to create new opportunities—and I'm not talking about retirement.

## Explaining Why Each Nonnegotiable Is Critical

Early in this chapter, we established that holding someone accountable is easier when you explain why a task is important. Providing a reason makes it easier for your team to accept what you are asking them to do. Without those reasons, buy-in will be slow, and you'll struggle to get the performance you need from your team. You must sell your salespeople your nonnegotiables, while also defending them from the holdouts who will try to delay, bend, or even break them.

Chapter 3 will help you communicate the same message over time without ever sounding like you are repeating yourself. Jeff Weiner, the former CEO of LinkedIn, once quoted David Gergen, an advisor to no less than four U.S. presidents: "History teaches that almost nothing a leader says is heard if spoken only once." As Weiner put it, quoting another colleague, "In order to effectively communicate to an audience, you need to repeat yourself so often that you grow sick of hearing yourself say it, and only then will people begin to internalize the message." (You can read Weiner's post on LinkedIn at https://www.linkedin .com/pulse/20140428141014-22330283-just-because-you-said-it-doesn-t-make-it-so/.)

## Commitment Is Greater Than Compliance

The reason you need buy-in for your vision and your nonnegotiable accountabilities is that you want *commitment* instead of *compliance*. Every year, you must pay your taxes, have your annual physical, and spend Thanksgiving with your Uncle Enrico, the conspiracy theorist who still tries to persuade you that we didn't land on the moon because we cannot escape the Van Allen belt. These are things you must do to be compliant, not because you are committed.

You want your team to commit to your vision, not just comply with it. You need them to enroll in new behaviors and beliefs because they understand how important they are to their results, their clients' success, and their company's growth. To remove compliance and replace it with commitment, you must identify and communicate the positive outcomes that accrue to those who do what is required of them.

Naturally, there are challenges you must overcome to secure this commitment. Forewarned is forearmed, so let's look at a couple of them.

## The Challenges of Uneven Commitment

One challenge of leadership is the uneven commitment you find in any group. As a leader, it is easier to communicate to your sales force as a group, treating them all the same. Bad idea! Different individuals often need something different from you, including different communication.

The challenge here is communicating to different groups and individuals based on their respective commitment or compliance. Those who are not committed should be addressed individually, to avoid implying that the committed individuals in a group are not.

You are better off taking the time to work with each individual than casting a wide net that treats the innocent the same as the guilty. Even though it's often more difficult, a personal appeal to an individual is more likely to result in a greater commitment than even speaking to the full group of holdouts, even though you will communicate both to your group and to individuals.

## The Difficulty of Behavioral Change

The reason individuals fail to contribute to revenue growth is that they don't take the actions that would generate those results. Some may not be committed, in which case you need to help them commit. Others may believe they should not have to do certain work, lack the competency to produce the outcome, or think they should be allowed to do what they prefer instead of what's needed.

In the end, you are going to have to engage holdouts to act. There will always be people on your team who believe what you say is good, right, and true while still refusing to do what you require of them. The strategy that has worked the best for me is simply to wear them down. (I am capable of talking for over three hours on a single breath, something that has caused my teenagers to voluntarily surrender their car keys to avoid another lecture about character and avoiding poor choices.)

## Implementing Humane Consequences

Without consequences, there is no accountability. Consequences should not start with ultimatums or threats, but with a light touch and a focus on improvement. As the leader, you want to use your influence to gain an individual's commitment, not force compliance. Your patience will reward you with a positive culture. Patience does not make pushovers—on the contrary, you are defending your standards, your nonnegotiables, and your revenue growth goals.

Requiring a meeting to review actions and outcomes is a good starting place. Asking an individual to develop an improvement plan and review it with you keeps them engaged, even though some will chafe at being asked to design such a plan. There may be a time to escalate, but you are better off continually asking

for commitment, especially when you haven't imposed consequences before now. Make this a long game and prove you will
not budge from your position.

While these challenges are real, you control the consistency of
your leadership. The second most common mistake leaders make
when establishing nonnegotiable actions and outcomes is not con-
stantly communicating their importance to their teams' results.
The most common mistake is not setting expectations and holding your team accountable, with an eye toward a positive culture.

# 8

## Structures of Accountability

THERE ARE STRUCTURES you can put in place to strengthen and maintain your positive culture of accountability. Instead of imposing and enforcing accountability yourself, you can release some of that responsibility to these structures—helping ensure your team creates the outcomes they are responsible for while you focus on reviewing their results.

When it comes to revenue growth, there are two paths to failure: not creating enough new opportunities and new clients, or not winning enough of them. Accordingly, to reach your goals and avoid these two pitfalls, your structures should enhance prospecting, creating net new opportunities, and acquiring new clients. Let's look at how they'll work.

## Self-Reporting

We have made a major mistake by relying on technology to track our sales force's activities and results. The larger and more complete your CRM dashboard, the more you prevent accountability. For instance, even when a team has a minimum quota for daily or weekly sales calls, few salespeople reach that level. They know that there are no consequences for not putting forth the effort to make, say, 20 outbound calls a day, proving that the dashboard is an obstacle when it comes to accountability. This approach prevents the salesperson from having to confront their lack of activity. A sales leader who says nothing about the low output is certain to get more of what they don't want, namely low activity.

Overemphasizing activity isn't the only way dashboards and CRM reports diminish accountability. Because you can see every opportunity in your team's pipeline, you know exactly where each salesperson is when it comes to their deals. Some of those deals have been "pending" for so long that they're practically toddlers. Perhaps you should give the responsible salesperson a cupcake with two candles, then have the whole office join in on a rousing rendition of "Happy Birthday to Your Deal." That, at least, might motivate them to start creating value for the prospective client before the little deal-let starts first grade.

Here is the major mistake we make when it comes to accountability: we allow salespeople to avoid reporting their own results, saying what they did and didn't do in the prior week. By not requiring them to articulate their progress, you spare them from the negative feelings that come from knowing they didn't do the work expected of them. The idea here isn't to shame any individual, but rather to make them confront their own behaviors. To separate accountability from (perceived) punishment, you can do two things. First, you can—and should—require everyone on your team to report their results. Second, you can enforce this requirement privately, as part of your weekly individual meetings.

Any meeting that requires a salesperson to report their own results helps improve their activity and their results. Even when you can already track poor results, it's important to make the salesperson deal with those results personally. But keep in mind what we learned last chapter about timing. Maintaining a professional standard means intervening as soon as you recognize an individual is creating a pattern of behavior that is harmful to them, to your team's results, and to your company. Ignoring problems effectively provides a waiver, making it more difficult for you to address the problem after you've let it go for weeks or even months.

If a goal is important enough to require accountability, it's important enough to allow self-reporting to help you maintain your standards.

## The Weekly Pipeline Meeting

The weekly pipeline meeting is a very important structure for accountability, in part because it forces the salesperson to report their results out loud, in front of their peers.

Different sales organizations have different ideas about when and how they should conduct a pipeline meeting. Most sales organizations review every opportunity in the pipeline, asking for a brief status update, while some look only at which deals have moved forward in the sales conversation. Not only are these meetings structured differently, but they're also on different time-lines: some teams meet every two weeks, others only monthly, and the ones that get the timing right meet every week.

By definition, a structure of accountability helps ensure the salesperson is generating the activity and outcomes they need. One of the reasons many sales forces don't generate enough opportunities is because they don't really hold people accounta-ble for creating those opportunities. When a salesperson doesn't generate enough opportunities, they clutter the pipeline with low-probability deals and opportunities that stopped deserving that name many months in the past. To be blunt, some sales managers feel better with a pipeline full of zombie deals. These deals look like they are alive, even though they expired long ago.

The weekly pipeline meeting is designed to create account-ability for creating net new opportunities. It isn't designed to talk through deal strategy, or to get a status update on every single deal. Because the focus of this meeting is very narrow, it can be conducted in a very short time with your entire team. You only need to do two things in this meeting: (1) get an accounting of each new opportunity each salesperson created in the last week, and (2) share any deal that moved forward in the past week.

The very best day to hold your pipeline meeting is Monday, and the best time to do it is at 4:30 p.m. It's a start of a new week, and each salesperson is going to account for their previous week. The weekly frequency discourages any salesperson from going two weeks without prospecting or creating new opportunities. That's already almost 4 percent of the entire year, and heaven forbid you allow a salesperson to lose a full month—as we all know, once you get past grade school, time always goes faster than you want it to. This is what we mean when we say, "the right work, at the right time, in the right way."

At one point in my career, I lost my three largest clients in short order. I had been living on these accounts, and I had not been prospecting. Why bother making all those cold calls, I thought, when I was generating the biggest commissions I'd ever received? And then before I could blink, the commissions were gone, and I had no pipeline. When I was later promoted to Vice President of Sales, I refused to let anyone on my team feel that way for lack of effort, so I used the pipeline meeting to verify everyone was creating new opportunities every week.

More specifically, during your pipeline meeting each person should describe out loud the new opportunities they created in the prior week, their potential revenue value, what the client is buying, and what their next step is. After sharing their new opportunities, they share which of their current deals have moved forward. The narrow content focus prevents anyone from being able to hide the fact that they haven't created any new opportunities in the prior week. It also prevents them from hiding behind a big deal they've been working on for months, a tactic almost always designed to avoid accountability for prospecting and creating new deals.

Revenue growth starts and ends with net new revenue, and a large part of that net new revenue will come from net new opportunities and the acquisition of new clients. Putting this structure in place helps ensure you have those new clients.

## Territory and Account Plans

Every salesperson on your team knows they're responsible for prospecting, even when they pretend otherwise. You probably already know which of your reps really do prospect and which ones are content to coast. Fortunately, you can improve your overall results in creating new opportunities by leveraging another structure of accountability, the territory and account plan.

Because your team already knows what prospecting means, you may not think that you must tell them what they need to do to prospect successfully. But in fact, you can improve your team's results by giving them strong direction on whom to target and how to go about prospecting. You gain net new opportunities by acquiring new logos, the new clients you need to ensure you reach your revenue goals. This is where territory plans come in.

You may have a few salespeople on your team who are happy living on the commissions from their existing clients. They hope they can grow those accounts and avoid having to win new logos. These salespeople can go years without any problems, only to be surprised when a client moves to a competitor, gets sold to another company, or decides to start filling your company's role in-house. Whatever the reason, the salesperson walks around, shell-shocked and stressed by their newly decapitated income. Because they haven't been prospecting, they are years away from replacing their very large client. You've churned a large client worth, let's say, $5,000,000. You now need $5,000,001 in new revenue to increase sales by $1.

Because we are interested in creating net new opportunities, part of every salesperson's work should also focus on creating opportunities *inside* their existing clients, something that requires an account plan. Imagine the salesperson who wins a new client and moves on immediately to win another client. They have little interest in growing their existing clients because they enjoy the chase more than maintaining a relationship. You need not prod or poke these salespeople to go acquire new logos, but you will have to push them to grow their existing clients. Otherwise, these salespeople will lose their accounts over time because they have no interest in creating new value, leaving the door wide open for a competitor to win a new logo by displacing you. Remember, churn is the devil. Not only does the client not grow, but you also lose all your existing revenue!

## Developing Territory and Account Plans

Because you want your team to prospect, you must require them to create a territory and account plan. This plan ensures they have done the work necessary to create the new opportunities—and in turn create new value for your existing clients and provide you with net new revenue. There is no greater retention strategy than caring enough to create new value.

Let's start with account plans. There are several components here your team should address:

- First, the salesperson needs to look at their existing clients, noting what they are currently buying from you.
- Using that data, they next need to determine how they could help the client improve their results and what initiative they should introduce next.
- The account plan will also benefit from having the salesperson identify who they are going to need to propose what they believe comes next, as well as which insights will answer the question "why change?"

When you assign a salesperson a territory, you likewise need them to learn that territory, identifying the companies that already buy what you sell or who would benefit from changing something they're doing. The first territory plan is always the most difficult, and it's almost always wrong, as the salesperson will need time to explore and learn their territory.

- Rank the clients by their revenue, starting with the largest clients and working their way toward the smaller ones.
- Identify the contacts they need to reach out to, including their phone number, mobile number, and email address.

- Capture the insights that make up something like an executive briefing the salesperson can use as a "value trade," making it easier to command a meeting with a decision-maker or decision-shaper.

Here's the key: because the salesperson created their account or territory plan, they are responsible for executing it. You are responsible for reviewing their plan to make sure it will produce net new opportunities and significant revenue. If there are prospective clients you believe the salesperson should prioritize, you can add those companies to the plan. It's your territory, after all, even if you have delegated it to your salesperson. You have a say in which clients they target and how they pursue them.

In your one-on-one meetings, you should refer to the salesperson's territory and account plans, asking them to update you on their progress. You can also expect new opportunities from the territory and account plans to show up during your pipeline meetings. This structure of accountability supports your pursuit of revenue growth. After putting it in place, you have an additional advantage with prospecting.

## Prospecting Sequences

To maximize the effectiveness of the previous two structures, make certain your sales force has an effective, consultative approach to prospecting. One of the best strategies you can execute is developing a prospecting sequence, a set of communications using multiple mediums, including some that provide insights and allow the salesperson to capture mindshare. You don't have to buy a fancy software program to use a sequence, and you should avoid any software that simply automates a series of emails—spam has never captured mindshare. Automation may be straightforward, but it is not personal and won't generate the right set of results.

The guardrails you provide here prevent the salesperson from making a single call to a prospective client in Q1 and not following up until Q3. When salespeople leave large gaps between attempts to acquire a meeting, they are not going to capture the client's mindshare, and they certainly won't gain a reputation as a reliable advisor who can improve their client's results. Your prospecting sequence should start with a general sequence, along with some principles you are going to ask your team to follow, should you allow them to customize their own sequences:

- The first principle is "phone first," because making a call and acquiring a meeting means the salesperson doesn't need seven or eight different touches. One person in a workshop asked me if sending eight emails over eight weeks was okay. I am certain none of the busy decision-makers your team is pursuing are looking for a pen-pal. Waiting two months to make a call is never a good decision.
- The second principle is "let them hear your voice," which means leaving a voicemail every time the salesperson calls. Otherwise, it's like knocking on their door and running away. Make certain the prospect knows the salesperson is trying to reach them.
- The third principle is never to ask the client to call you back. Instead, have the salesperson say they will call the client back the next day. It isn't the prospect's responsibility to follow up with the salesperson; that's the salesperson's job.
- The fourth principle is to send an email that trades value for the client's time (i.e., to read the email) without asking for a meeting or even a response. Instead, the email should state that salesperson will call the client back the next day.

- The fifth principle is to make a good number of touches, "no ask" communications—for example, printing an article, highlighting the money line, and handwriting a note explaining why it's important models the act of providing advice even before the client meets with the salesperson. We call these "no ask" communications because they are a way to provide value before claiming any.

The great value of a professional sequence is its emphasis on the patient, professional persistence necessary to eventually score a meeting. Salespeople learn that they must stay "top of mind" with their clients by providing the type of insights that show they are also on top of the challenges, problems, and obstacles the client is either experiencing now or soon will be. A sequence can also allow you to arm your team with a narrative that explains all that is going on in the prospect's world, increasing the likelihood of gaining a meeting.

## Quarterly Internal Business Review

You now have your team self-reporting and increasing their activity, even if a few came along kicking and screaming. You are also now conducting weekly pipeline meetings focused on net new opportunities created in the prior week. Your territory and account plans are in place, and you are supporting the acquisition of new clients with a prospecting sequence that increases your team's activity while also positioning them as consultative experts.

The final structure of accountability is the Quarterly Internal Business Review. This meeting is going to require each salesperson to report their results in the last quarter before sharing what changes they are going to make going into the next quarter. Both you and your team will recognize how different your quarter looks compared to before you put these structures in place. In simple terms, these structures are a set of disciplines that help you create net new opportunities, win new clients, and generate net new revenue in excess of your churn.

Each person on your team needs to report on the status of the major accounts where they were able to create new opportunities and generate new revenue. They also need to report on the new clients they acquired in the period and the new revenue they generated or expect to generate. They should have learned several things while working in their territory, like which competitors own what clients, as well as who the decision-makers are in the companies they are pursuing.

You hope each salesperson learns something that will help them improve in the future, situating them to share tribal knowledge that would also help their teammates improve their results. You want to know what each individual will do differently, as well as what they believe they need to do more of. In this way, you've moved beyond simply holding each individual salesperson responsible for their results. They are now accountable to each other, since they have each contributed to crafting a positive culture of accountability.

# 9

## People

YOUR RESULTS WILL never exceed your sales force's effectiveness. Here we confront the age-old question: Are good salespeople born or made? The answer is yes, some salespeople are born with certain attributes that make selling something natural to them. And yes, salespeople are also made—by training, coaching, and lots of hard work—and succeed even without the indefinable *je ne sais quoi* of sales acumen.

When I was 19, I had a job in my family's staffing business, interviewing candidates for light industrial positions in warehouses, manufacturing plants, and other positions that required manual labor. Some days I interviewed 15 or 20 people. Later, after I transferred to a larger company in Los Angeles, I interviewed as many as 40 people in a day. Over the five years I did that job, I probably interviewed over ten thousand people.

To be fair, these were not overly long interviews, but I still developed a sense about who would do well and who would not even show up for their assignment. One day, the intimidating senior vice president of my company, Peter Margarita, watched me walk back and forth in front of the conference room where he was meeting with his branch managers. Noticing how fast I was interviewing people, he called me into the room to question me about why I wasn't using the company's approved process.

I explained that I was being courteous by doing quick interviews with some candidates, knowing I wouldn't be able to help them, so I could spend more time with the people I could place in actual jobs. To my relief, Peter smiled and told his managers, "This is how I expect our people to think." I left the room sweating, grateful I had dodged a bullet.

If I could somehow transfer my sixth sense about hiring and professional development through this book, I would gladly do so. It's nothing I can explain, except to say that it is something that developed in my subconscious mind. But I can tell you how to improve your ability to hire and develop salespeople.

The process starts with a competency model, which you can use to help direct your interview and get a sense of whether an applicant has a chance of succeeding in a position.

## The Competency Model

Most sales organizations lack a competency model, a set of character traits and skills they believe are necessary for success in the role they are trying to fill. Without a competency model, you cannot be a good interviewer and you'll be making uninformed hiring decisions. My competency model includes a rather long list of character traits and skills. Some may be relevant to your organization's hiring decisions and others might not be, so you can download a scorecard, which you can customize, at www .thesalesblog.com/leadinggrowth.

You will notice right away that there are more character traits than skills. While skills are important, I would suggest that character traits count for much more when it comes to results. This is because people can, in most cases, learn or improve skills that would improve their performance, but it is much more difficult to help someone to change or develop character traits.

Most sales managers believe they are hiring for skills and experience. But when they must fire a salesperson, it's more likely because of a character deficit than a skill deficit. As you read through these two lists, you will understand why some salespeople no longer work for you. You'll also have strong hunches about who on your team right now is going to need some help.

### Character Traits

A few of the character traits in my competency model are dealbreakers for me, meaning if they're missing, I know I won't hire the individual. Notably, I refuse to hire people who lack self-discipline:

if I must ask you to do your work, we are not long for each other. I'd rather pass on the individual than have them fail because they can't even keep the commitments they make to themselves.

- **Self-Discipline.** Self-discipline is the ability to keep your commitments—to yourself and others. I can get a sense of an individual's discipline by asking them what time they get out of bed each morning and having them share with me what they do in the first couple of hours they're awake. You can also ask about their workday to discern whether they are disciplined.
- **Optimism.** Attitude is key. A person who is negative or pessimistic is not likely to do well in sales to start with, but the greater threat is that they'll spread their negativity to other members of your team, especially those who are struggling. Ask a candidate how they deal with rejection and what bothers them to get a better sense of how they deal with negative events. If they believe they are being personally rejected when a client says no, ask why they believe that. After all, the client only rejected the meeting request.
- **Emotional Intelligence.** Emotional intelligence includes self-awareness. It's sometimes called EQ, which stands for *emotional quotient* (like IQ, or intelligence quotient). Selling well requires having the emotional intelligence to recognize your buyer's state and their perspective. But it also means recognizing your own state and how others perceive you. Great salespeople will project this in an interview, but remember that, in that situation, you're the buyer and they're selling you on hiring them. It's something you can forget when a good candidate engages with you.
- **Caring.** Selling is an other-oriented endeavor, meaning good salespeople care about others. This is particularly important in consultative sales, which requires learning about your client so you can be a good advisor—even if you don't think you'll make

a sale right away. People who are self-oriented repel clients. Though they don't realize they're projecting that the deal is more about their commission check than the client's success, a small whiff of their self-orientation is enough to turn clients off.

- **Street Smarts.** Having street smarts means being savvy and shrewd. It's difficult to take advantage of or manipulate a shrewd person, but they can often use that shrewdness to identify and provide value to others.

- **Ability to Read People.** The ability to understand what someone wants or needs is one key to providing it. Each person prefers a certain currency: some like recognition, some power, and some certainty. When you can intuit your buyer's needs and motivations, you have a distinct advantage in creating a preference to buy from you.

- **Competitiveness.** Because selling is a competition, it helps to hire people who are competitive by nature. People who have a burning desire to win (but not that they're *entitled* to win) will work harder to beat their competition. Ask candidates about what it means to win a new client over a competitor.

- **Resourcefulness.** You need to hire people who can figure things out on their own. Whether or not you have children, you don't need your employees to be your dependents. They shouldn't ask you what to do without even trying to come up with a solution on their own. Ask candidates about a time they were stuck, and what they did about it.

- **Initiative.** Initiative and resourcefulness go hand in hand. In a role with autonomy, you want to hire someone who will be proactive, never waiting for directions. Ask candidates about areas in which they should take initiative, or times when they acted before it was necessary.

- **Persistence.** Make sure your candidate isn't the kind that gives up too easily. I have never understood why salespeople believe a client "rejected them" when they asked for a meeting.

The client only rejected their pitch for a meeting. You want to hire someone who believes "no" is simply feedback that causes them to adjust and try again.

- **Communication.** Effective communication requires listening. It's important that a salesperson thinks well on their feet and has excellent talk tracks—but it's even more important that they're a great listener. Assess your candidate on how well they are retaining what you've told them.

- **Accountability.** Good employees own the outcomes they are responsible for. No client will be happy with a salesperson who happily provides a contract but disappears at the first sign of trouble. Ask candidates what they have done when a client wasn't getting the results they promised.

- **Authenticity.** There is no question here: salespeople need to be comfortable with who they are. Being uncomfortable can look like a lack of confidence. Judge your potential rep on how easy it is for them to be real and authentic.

- **Confidence.** You are better off hiring someone who is a little overconfident (without being arrogant) than someone who lacks confidence. It's difficult to take advice and recommendations from someone who isn't sure of themselves. During your interview, note how confidently your candidate makes their argument. Do they believe in themselves? If not, no one else is going to either.

- **Courage.** Courage goes hand in hand with confidence. To determine if your candidate is courageous, you can challenge one of their answers and watch their response. For example, ask, "Is that what you think is the best way to prospect?" If they defend their answer or ask you what's better, you have evidence that they are comfortable with conflict. Because business comes with some amount of conflict, you want someone who can handle it comfortably and professionally. They should come across as confident and open to hearing an opposing view, not as either belligerent or overly willing to back down.

- **Diplomacy.** Challenging a candidate is also a good way to measure their diplomacy, meaning their ability to be measured and polite. Even if they disagree, they should be able to do so respectfully.
- **Curiosity.** Modern salespeople need to be curious. When your role includes teaching your client and helping them with a paradigm shift, you want to hire people who have a desire to learn and discover. Ask them what they are reading, listening to, or studying. The longer it takes them to answer this question, the more it is unlikely they are naturally curious.
- **Sense of Humor.** Of course, not everyone shares the same idea of what is funny. But you are not looking for a comedian as much as someone who can engage and entertain clients in a conversation.
- **Passion.** A person that is passionate about something tends to be a person who can give themselves over to their work. They are invariably more interesting and more engaged. Most candidates will tell you that they're dedicated to their work, so try asking, "What are you passionate about outside of work?"
- **Success Orientation.** This is one of my top three character traits. (Remember, my default leadership style is laissez-faire.) Often described as hunger, success orientation means you'll never need to motivate the individual because they're already intrinsically motivated. On a plane ride to Phoenix, I met a senior sales leader from a large technology company. As we were talking shop, he told me he only hires salespeople who are "crisp." I didn't have to ask him to describe "crisp" because I was looking at it.

Imagine a salesperson who checks enough of the character trait boxes that you are comfortable hiring them. There may be other traits that suggest the candidate you are interviewing is a good fit. *Fit* is sometimes considered a vague, nebulous quality, but all it really means is that a person has the potential to succeed in the position you're hiring them for. Assessing an interviewee's character traits gives you a concrete way to determine that.

## The Skills

Knowing your potential salesperson has great character traits, you next must consider whether they have the skills they need to succeed in the job. It's unlikely that a candidate will check all these boxes, so you'll also have to determine if you can help them acquire any skills they're missing.

- **Closing.** I have always believed that closing, the ability to gain commitments, is the most critical sales skill. The first contact with a prospective client is a request for a meeting. Because the linear concept of the sales process is now broken, every salesperson needs to ask and acquire a series of commitments. Ask your candidate to role-play a request for a meeting with you.
- **Consultative.** It's important for a B2B salesperson to provide counsel, advice, and recommendations to their clients. Ask your could-be new salesperson about the best advice they ever gave a client and how it helped the client improve their results. Hopefully that advice will go beyond "buy my solution from my company," but you may be disappointed. It is likely you will have to develop the ability to consult.
- **Objection-Handling.** How a person handles any objection can give you insight into how they will resolve client concerns. All you need to do to discover how a salesperson responds to an objection is to say, "I am concerned that your background might not have prepared you for this role." Your candidate will be thrown for a loop, having never been challenged in an interview. If they make a serious attempt to defend themselves and address your concern, they're worth considering.

- **Prospecting.** Salespeople need the ability to create opportunities. The way to assess prospecting is to ask the candidate how they schedule a meeting with a client, and how they turn that meeting into an opportunity. Ask them to describe how they primarily book meetings. You are praying for the answer, "I call them." Personally, my rule is *no phone, no job.*

- **Storytelling.** In a modern sales approach, it's important for a salesperson to control the narrative, especially when it comes to helping clients change. They need to be able to describe the future in a compelling way. You can check for this skill in many ways, such as asking the candidate to tell you a story about the biggest deal they ever won (or lost) and what they learned.

- **Diagnosis (Eliciting the Root Cause of a Challenge).** For me, this is a hurdle higher than some other skills. If a salesperson was trained in a legacy approach, they are almost certain to talk about eliciting the client's problem. I don't care about "the problem" as much as I do its root cause, since knowing (and engaging) that cause is a prerequisite for being consultative. Ask candidates about the common problems they helped solve, what the root causes of the problems were, and how they addressed them.

- **Questioning.** Salespeople need to be able to ask powerful questions, meaning those that reframe a client objection or concern. This prompts clients to think beyond the comfort of the status quo. Here is a powerful question: "Would it be better for you to change on your terms and your timeline instead of being forced to change on a timeline that isn't good for your business?" Don't expect that level when you ask candidates if they have any questions. But if all they do is ask you about pay and benefits, they may need help with questions. You hope to get a question like: "What do you expect over the first 90 days?"

- **Differentiating.** At the heart of differentiation is the ability to create a preference. When you ask a question designed to determine if a candidate can do this, you will probably not get a good answer. The person you are interviewing has likely been taught and trained to believe their company and their solution is the differentiation. You will have to help them understand how to differentiate themselves in the sales conversation. This skill can be taught, especially if a person has the character traits on the competency model.
- **Negotiating.** More disappointment is likely here. When a prospective client asks the salesperson for a lower price, most salespeople will tell the client they will go back to speak to their manager and see what they can do. That tells you that the salesperson is negotiating on behalf of the client, even though they ostensibly work for you. You must train them to immediately, and without hesitation, ask for something from the client. This is the way to reach win–win deals.
- **Business Acumen.** This includes professional insights and the ability to create value. When you hire a mature, experienced salesperson, expect them to have significant business acumen. A younger, greener hire will need help becoming a businessperson so they can develop into a business advisor.
- **Change Management.** Change management—the ability to build consensus—needs to be taught, but it rarely appears on anyone's development plan. The best you can do here is ask the salesperson to tell you about big deals and how many people were part of a deal they won. It's good if they have had to deal with multiple stakeholders, but you can expect to do some work here.
- **Leadership.** Salespeople need to lead the client. How could it be otherwise when they must provide them with advice about their business? The more the candidate can lead, the more likely they'll be a good salesperson. Leadership is what drives results that involve others.

# The Two Ways You Acquire Talent

There are only two ways you can acquire talent. The first way is to buy it. Even though it is difficult to do, you need to always stay aware of salespeople interested in leaving their current position. You can track salespeople you've met and monitor their LinkedIn profiles. Also, tell any salesperson that impresses you to connect with you and provide them with your phone number. When you buy talent, you can expect fast results. You have paid so you don't have to wait for them to develop.

The second way to acquire the talent you need is to build individuals. The young salesperson who is too green to be good—but has all the right traits—provides you with the opportunity to develop them, eliminating some of the bad beliefs and behaviors that will limit their success. It's more work to hire, teach, train, and develop a salesperson, but by not building the talent you need, you will miss out on great salespeople who develop under your charge.

The best way to acquire the talent you need is to use both strategies. When you can buy the talent, hire a successful salesperson, even if they haven't worked in your industry. We often try to hire from our industry because we don't want to teach new employees the business. That isn't a good reason to turn an inexperienced salesperson away. When you find a person you believe can grow into the role, hire them, and spend the time to develop them.

# How to Select Whom You Should Interview

Sort the resumes into three piles. The first pile is your A pile, representing the people with the right background and results that identify them as someone with great potential. Candidates in the second pile, the B pile, are missing something you'd want to see. The C pile holds the resumes of people without skills and experience you'd want to see, but there is evidence that they have succeeded, starting in high school and through college. This group of people is commonly overlooked, but often contains people you'd love to hire.

Because you need to make a carefully considered decision when hiring, you need to interview many people. You will never have enough time to interview every candidate you believe might work, so let me suggest a way to solve this problem.

Schedule a 15-minute phone interview with your candidates in all three piles, starting with the A candidates. Often you will be disappointed within the first five minutes, which at least tells you that you don't need a longer interview. For instance, I once asked a potential hire to tell me what he would need to succeed in the new role I was hiring for. He requested a product that everyone wants to buy that is designed to ensure he would have so many leads that he could just take their orders. Schedule the candidates who make it through all 15 minutes for a real interview.

You will be tempted to skip the B and C piles. Let me convince you otherwise. When you hire a person, you want to make certain that you want to work with this person every day. Follow the same process for the B and C resumes. When I discovered that I would have to work with the person I hired, I changed my mind about how important it was that I wanted to work with them. I once hired a salesperson with all the right skills and experience, but there was something about him that prevented us from connecting, and neither of us really wanted to work with the other.

One more thing: the most important party in your hiring decision is your prospective clients. Some part of your calculation must include how you believe your clients will take to the person you are hiring. If the person you are considering was a salesperson in their previous roles, ask them to put you in touch with a few clients they acquired. You can ask the client about their experience with the person you are considering.

## You Are Hiring a Person's Weaknesses

One reason sales leaders make poor hiring decisions is that they only try to identify the person's strengths. But it's more important to identify the person's weaknesses. Every person that sits across from you in an interview has both strengths and weaknesses. A good hiring decision is based on your ability to live with their weaknesses, or better still, help shore them up.

It's easier to train and teach skills than it is to instill character traits. It's easier to live with a lack of skills than a lack of character traits, but you will discover everyone has missing elements from both lists. If we're honest with ourselves, we would recognize that we are perfect exactly the way we are—and that we could use some improvement. After all, you just picked up a book you believe will help you improve your ability to create revenue growth.

## The First Priority Is Sales Effectiveness

There is no greater priority than sales effectiveness to enhance revenue growth. A highly effective salesperson will have an easier time scheduling meetings with their dream clients. Their effectiveness in a first meeting allows them to create a new opportunity. No matter whom you hire, you must reject the illusion that your sales force already possesses the maximum effectiveness they are capable of. Instead, you must see something in each person they cannot yet see themselves and use that insight to help them unleash their full potential.

The competency model in this chapter provides you with a lens through which to identify the areas where improving a salesperson's effectiveness will cause an equal improvement in their results. Your awareness of that potential makes you a good coach, one capable of helping the salesperson take the opportunity to improve their effectiveness.

Most salespeople on your team were likely trained in legacy approaches designed and developed for a time and market long past. It's likely they have never been provided a modern approach, so they'll be missing at least a few of the competency model's skills. Specifically, you can be certain they are not prepared to provide insights, leverage their business acumen, create value for the client inside the sales conversation, manage change, build consensus, and lead their contacts, decision-makers, and stakeholders. You can find resources about effectiveness at www.thesalesblog.com/leadinggrowth.

## Putting Everyone on a Plan

There is no reason to put a person on an improvement plan after they are already failing, just as there's no reason to close the barn door after the horses are already long gone. Because we often pretend that every salesperson we hire is effective enough, we don't do enough to help them develop to their full potential. Different people need to improve in different areas; everyone is a fixer-upper. Individual development calls, of course, for individual development plans. When it comes to transforming your team's approach from an outdated, legacy approach to a modern approach, though, everyone needs the same development simultaneously.

On surveys, salespeople state that they want more coaching from their sales manager, and for good reason, too: selling has changed more in the last few years than any other time in modern history. The opportunity here, at least for those who understand how important sales effectiveness is to their results, is to execute a long-term plan to develop everyone on their team. When different people have different needs at different times, putting your salesperson on a plan means giving them the individual attention they need, helping them to prioritize whichever trait or skill will allow them to level up.

Occasionally, some smart founder comes up with a product or service so much better than anything else in their category that they dominate the market. The best example may be Steve Jobs and the iPhone, a device that eventually destroyed the two largest phone manufacturers. Travis Kalanick and Garett Camp started Uber and likewise changed transportation, making it difficult for one to consider a taxi after downloading the app. These are market disruptors, and they are rare in B2B sales.

Most of us in B2B and B2C sales live in the Red Ocean, with products and services (across companies) similar enough that what we sell is often treated as a commodity. In Red Ocean industries, it's difficult to create a sustainable advantage that creates enough differentiation by itself to dominate the market. Instead, you will find your advantage through sales effectiveness supremacy, the ability to be the best sales organization in your category. When selling is a variable in your results, investing time and money into improving your team can create a sustainable competitive advantage.

# 10

---

## Effectiveness

FOR A NUMBER of years, I've been imploring sales leaders to make sales effectiveness their number-one initiative, especially at the start of the year. The greater your force's effectiveness, the greater your growth. You may be able to buy some of the talent you need, but the rest you'll need to build. The mistake that most sales leaders make is accepting their sales force's current effectiveness level, never prioritizing the initiatives that would increase their ability to both create and win the new opportunities necessary to grow their revenue. Here we need to add another formula for growth:

Sales Force's Effectiveness = Revenue Growth Rate

Imagine you have ten salespeople on your team. What impact would it have on your revenue to lose your top two producers? I'm sure it would be a challenge to make up for their contributions. One approach to that challenge is to add two new stars to your team who can be as effective as the two you lost. While I don't oppose that strategy, it's not the only one. Instead, improving your results means improving the effectiveness of each individual on your team. This maximizes your results by ensuring you get everything you can out of every person on your team.

## The Technology Trap

I have seen far too many sales leaders turn to technology to improve the sales force's "efficiency," building large, expensive sales stacks made up of software their sales team doesn't use. One company I know has a sales stack that costs them $7,000 per salesperson per year. Arming their 200 salespeople costs the company close to $1.5 million annually.

In the last year, two companies I know decided to implement a new CRM, taking their entire sales team out of the field to work on transferring and auditing their records. Projects like this may be important, but they don't hold a candle to the deals they lost while their team gave their time and effort to the new CRM.

These salespeople would have preferred to be in the field, and the time they lost on this project threatened their goals and did nothing to create revenue growth.

When it comes to sales and revenue growth, worry less about technological efficiency and more about your team's sales effectiveness. No one buys from you because you have a very expensive, if underutilized, sales stack. Nor will a new CRM differentiate you from your competition. While it's important to arm your team with the right technologies, and vital to have an effective CRM, they simply don't contribute to effectiveness.

## The Master Key to Revenue Growth Is Effectiveness

The greater your effectiveness, the greater your results. The greater your results, the greater your revenue growth. Unfortunately, the opposite is equally true: the more ineffective the sales force, the poorer your results. Poor results prevent revenue growth and may cause you to create what some people call "negative growth," a handy euphemism for "shrinking revenue."

Since the beginning of time, sales managers have looked to increase activity to improve their sales results. I can imagine a merchant on the Silk Road some 2,000 years ago, lambasting the assistant who helped them drag their wares over hundreds of miles, complaining that the assistant needs to have more conversations with the people who walk in front of their tent at the bazaar. It is doubtful any such merchants asked their assistants to improve their sales conversation, since it's much easier to demand more activity.

The idea that "more" is somehow better than "better" is seductive, as it doesn't require the sales leader to figure out how to increase their team's effectiveness by changing their beliefs and their behaviors. The only time more activity is the right solution to a revenue problem is when there is too little activity from an already highly effective sales force. Asking salespeople who are not yet effective to double, triple, or even quadruple their activity means wasting effort and annoying your prospective clients, who expect the salesperson to be competent enough to help them improve their results. One sales leader I know believed that his small team just needed to make more phone calls. Because he couldn't help them improve, they became frustrated, and one by one they all left the company. Instead of more deals, he lost his job and was replaced with a sales leader who knew how to improve results.

Increasing your team's effectiveness needs to precede any increase in activity, so your new activity can generate results that would not have been possible with an ineffective sales force. Reversing the order and increasing activity first produces too few results for the effort.

Waste not, want not. Imagine a sales force that wins a little less than 20 percent of their opportunities. To reach their revenue goal, their leader requires them to create a pipeline four times larger than the one they have now. Panicked, the sales force did exactly what was asked of them, creating a pipeline of low-probability opportunities, many of which weren't even real, let alone probable wins. The leader has what they believe to be a pipeline large enough to reach their goal. However, that pipeline lacks integrity, and the few deals that have potential are still being pursued by ineffective salespeople who will be challenged to bring them across the line.

Some sales leaders believe a large pipeline is the most important factor when it comes to revenue growth. Why a sales manager would somehow believe that quadrupling a pipeline would increase their team's win rate from 20 percent to, say, 35 percent is beyond me. Prioritizing sales effectiveness is the key to capitalizing on the opportunities any sales force creates. Leaders who believe a greater pipeline is the only metric they need to improve underestimate how much time it takes to build that pipeline, time that would be better spent on the high-visibility, high-value, must-win deals that speed you toward your goal.

## How to Improve Effectiveness

It's easy to recognize that the top 20 percent of your sales force will carry a large portion of your revenue growth. Some sales-people will have the attributes and skills (see Chapter 9) that make it relatively easy to succeed, while their colleagues must try harder to put up average numbers or even to sell at all. Selling has never been easy, but it is infinitely more difficult now, especially for those who have not been taught and trained how to sell effectively.

It's tempting to plot your team members on a standard bell curve and accept that you will always have 20 percent top producers, 20 percent strugglers, and 60 percent around the median. Improving your effectiveness means never settling for standard. Instead, you must develop your team's effectiveness to pull their curve to the right and create a "fat tail" in the graph.

Imagine you have a normal bell curve that is perfectly centered on a piece of paper or floating on your computer screen. You have a line showing the top 20 percent of your sales force on the far right. On the far left, you have the bottom 20 percent, the salespeople who are struggling because they are new or are not effective enough to contribute to growth. On the left of the center line, you have the 30 percent of the sales force that is under the median. On the right side of that line, of course, you have the 30 percent that is above the median.

If everyone on your team improves their effectiveness and their results, the entire bell curve will move to the right. The best get a little bit better, boosting their performance. Those on either side of the median will make a greater contribution to revenue growth, as will those at the tail end of the bell curve. Even though there will be some who move up to a different category, you'll still have a bottom 20 percent. But that bottom 20 percent will have produced more revenue than they did before you increased their effectiveness.

Let's assume the first bell curve produced $50 million of revenue. After your effectiveness initiative takes hold, you generate $55 million of revenue, a 10 percent increase. The only variable driving that progress is the higher effectiveness. Now, the increases for individual salespeople won't follow a linear model: salespeople who are already effective tend to make greater gains than less effective salespeople. For instance, a top producer who delivered $8 million in revenue before they increased their effectiveness might now produce $9.2 million, while a poor performer who was only able to squeak out $200K in revenue now generates $400K in revenue. That's a 100 percent increase, even if the revenue is still nowhere near their target.

While your competitors build a gigantic sales tech stack, believing their gains come from efficiency, you must focus on winning the new deals that deliver net new revenue. It is neither necessary nor right to look at your team's current performance and believe they can't get better. The best leaders see something in individuals that they don't yet see in themselves. Each member of your team has greater potential than either one of you can imagine—something you'll recognize if you have ever had a great leader, coach, mentor, or parent. All things being equal, your win rate is the one metric that provides you with the clearest view of effectiveness.

## Building a Fat-Tail Distribution

There is another type of curve you might strive for, one that looks a lot different than the traditional bell curve. Instead of the giant hump right in the middle of the graph, imagine the hump skewed to the right, leaving only a little tail just past the center line. Now instead of having 20 percent of top performers followed by the next 30 percent bordering the midline, you have 70 percent of the sales force to the right of the center line and only 30 percent left of center.

In the first example, you build your bell curve based on the ranking of each individual's percentage of revenue. On the fat-tail curve, you plot individuals by their actual revenue. This curve allows more people to find themselves right of center. I happen to have a fat-tail distribution with a small team, with four of six salespeople to the right of center, the result of having an incredibly effective sales force.

## The Starting Point for Greater Effectiveness

The starting point for improving and increasing your sales effectiveness is using the right sales approach to pursue your strategy. As the world has become more complex, the two legacy approaches to B2B sales are losing their efficacy, since most clients don't find they create as much value as they once did.

The oldest of the legacy approaches has been practiced for more than five decades, and maybe longer. It's a fear-based approach that is at odds with the current environment, one in which the salesperson needs to lead their clients and provide real and valuable insights. Even the "new and improved" legacy solution approach is closing in on four decades. It too has been completely commoditized, as every sales organization using the problem-pain-solution approach tries to differentiate themselves in exactly the same way: Rapport, Company History, Logo Slide, Our Solutions, What's keeping you up at night?

The whole point of differentiation is to create a preference to buy from you. Even though your product, your service, your solution, or the way you deliver value after you acquire a client may differ starkly from your competitors, the sales conversation is the only vehicle you have to win the client's business.

To differentiate your company and the value you create, you must start by providing a sales conversation that stands out and creates more value for your contacts. The modern sales approach is designed to do just that. It's an insight-based approach, one that provides the context for your conversation while also compelling change. Your insights provide the client with a better understanding of their environment while also helping them discover something about themselves, their business, and what they need to address to improve their results. By doing so, you seek to lead your clients, facilitating the buyer's journey and influencing the mechanisms of a nonlinear sales process.

## How to Develop Your Sales Force's Effectiveness

Updating your sales approach, to align it with what your prospective clients want and need from your sales force, is the best place to begin increasing your team's overall effectiveness. As helpful as the modern approach is, though, it isn't enough by itself. You have to do the work to develop your sales force. Each of the components we'll go through are necessary, and together they create a comprehensive approach to developing effectiveness. Let's look at each of the component parts before we plan a curriculum.

### Sales Training for Effectiveness

The reason check-box sales training fails is because it is treated as a one-time event, typically something you do in the course of a single day. Over the course of six hours, a trainer provides strategies, tactics, and talk tracks for a major concept. The sales trainer has to have perfect delivery and the ability to transfer competency to a group of people who are seeing the content for the first time. In turn, the salespeople need to have perfect comprehension, perfect execution, and perfect retention after experiencing the content exactly once.

It is one thing to transfer knowledge; it is quite different to transfer competency. Effectiveness is only made possible by competency transfer. The best approach to training a sales force is to commit to training weekly, covering a new aspect of sales every two weeks. In the first week, you provide a short training on that aspect, ensuring your team acquires the knowledge by requiring them to explain how and when they are going to use it in the following week. At the end of the second week, you require each person on your team to explain how they used what they learned, what worked, what didn't work, and how they might change what they did to improve their results.

By prioritizing the areas where your team needs development, you can start increasing your team's overall effectiveness in ways that will make an immediate impact on revenue growth. You may want to spend more than two weeks on certain character traits or sales skills, increasing your team's competency for producing an outcome that improves their ability to succeed. If your team needs more time to practice in roleplays and in the field, give them the time. Development isn't a race, and you should not be concerned about efficiency when what you want is competency and effectiveness.

## Coaching Individuals to Improve Effectiveness

Treat every interaction with a salesperson as a chance to provide coaching. You may never have enough time to give every team member the kind of structured, detailed coaching they need. But you can still use the same two-week cadence to fit coaching on your calendar, perhaps by giving every salesperson 30 minutes of individual coaching. A sales manager with 10 salespeople might need to provide two and half hours of coaching each week.

Training and development don't always increase an individual's effectiveness, because different individuals need help in areas outside of training. Coaching provides the opportunity to help improve an individual's effectiveness by addressing the specific challenges and obstacles that prevent them from reaching their targets and contributing to revenue growth. Coaching is also designed to improve the salesperson's competency, requiring the salesperson to change their beliefs and their behaviors. A coaching session in one week should be followed by a week to practice in the field. If the individual needs more time, let them continue to work on competency.

## Transferring Tribal Knowledge and Increasing Effectiveness

There is a different dynamic at play when you bring your team together to share what's working and what's not. One way to transfer the mindset, strategies, and tactics that lead to success is to review an opportunity as a group that provides some important lesson.

You start by identifying an opportunity that allows you to highlight some important idea or strategy or tactic. Ask the salesperson involved to talk through their opportunity, explaining something they did that worked or a novel workaround for some obstacle. By listening to this account, the rest of the sales force acquires "tribal knowledge" they can use in similar sales scenarios. That will naturally encourage them to ask questions about this case study, to better understand what they might be able to do to develop and win their own deals.

This approach is a minimal viable development approach. It doesn't require you to take your sales force out of the field for long periods, nor does it require them to do long homework assignments. It provides you, as the sales leader, with a plan you can execute, and one that isn't going to dominate your calendar.

## Enabling Effectiveness in the Modern Sales Approach

I began this book with the idea a salesperson must create two outcomes to create net new revenue: creating opportunities and capturing opportunities. Your development plan should increase your team's competency for both of these outcomes. Let's start by looking at how you develop a sales force with a high level of competency at creating new opportunities.

*Effectiveness in Opportunity Creation*

Developing the following five core sales competencies will improve your effectiveness and increase the number—and quality—of your team's opportunities.

1. **Philosophy of Value.** Your sales force needs to understand what clients need in the way of results. My own approach is called Level 4 Value Creation (L4VC™), a model with two big advantages. First, it starts the conversation with (1) the strategic outcomes the client needs, and (2) a theory about the challenges that prevent them from producing those outcomes. Second, L4VC™ enables the sales force to engage in a sales conversation that differentiates the salesperson and their company by creating greater value than their competitors. You need a philosophy of value to support your approach.

2. **Building Insights.** To field a sales force that can create value for your clients in the sales conversation, you need to build the insights that help those clients understand their world and the root cause of their challenges and their poor results. A salesperson who can teach the client something valuable and provide them with a higher-resolution lens through which to view their current state and their potential future state is one who can win the client's trust moving forward. This is the very heart of a modern sales approach.

3. **Consultative Prospecting.** In the past, prospecting meant smiling and dialing. But today it is necessary to provide an approach that is more consultative. Using discovery only to tell a client about your company, products, and services is

at odds with the fact that buyers can find most of that info on your website. Pitching a meeting now requires a valuable proposition capable of enticing a decision-maker to trade you their time, something you enable by understanding what clients value and by providing them with insights and a new perspective. Consultative prospecting is enabled by a sequence of communications that prove the salesperson is worth a meeting.

4. **Commitment Gaining.** Sales is a series of conversations and commitments to future conversations. A salesperson who cannot consistently acquire commitments to future meetings will have no end of problems pursuing deals. Most sales organizations need to address multiple client needs over the course of several meetings. The key to acquiring the commitments you need is creating enough value in the current meeting that your prospective client will eagerly agree to another session.

5. **Advanced Discovery.** The traditional approach to discovery is about extracting a confession from the client, one that allows the salesperson to recognize their problem (as if they didn't already know it). By contrast, a modern approach is one in which the client also makes a series of discoveries. Advanced discovery means that both the salesperson and the client are learning from each other, exploring the client's future potential and the changes they might need to make.

## Effectiveness in Opportunity Capture

From here, we need to look at four major competencies that increase effectiveness in pursuing and capturing those opportunities:

1. **Handling Objections.** There are always going to be obstacles that prevent clients from moving forward. We have always

had to "handle objections," but a better way to understand these objections is by looking at them as real concerns that the client isn't willing to disclose. By dealing with the client's real concerns, you can help your client remove the obstacles and continue on their path to better results.

2. **Presentations and Proposals.** Most presentations and proposals start with "why us," with the salesperson walking (or at least dragging) the client through all the reasons why the client should buy from them. This legacy approach isn't consultative. A better approach begins by reminding your contacts of the reasons they need to change, followed by the future outcomes they need to reach, before explaining exactly how you and your contacts are going to make this change. The "why us" follows the investment as a way to explain your company's commitment and establish the resources they'll use to ensure success.

3. **Building Consensus.** In deals of all sizes, you will need to help your clients build consensus within their organization, so they can collectively consent to the change you are helping them make. Most companies lack a framework and the competency necessary to deal with the difficult, sometimes political, process of aligning around any change initiative. This competency is much more difficult than most of the others, and it requires much more attention than most sales organizations give it.

4. **Mastering Negotiations.** You can expect every client to ask your sales force to sharpen their pencil and write down a discounted price. You can also expect your salespeople to tell their prospective client that they'll ask you what they can do. What they really mean is that they are going to negotiate a concession with you that they can give their client, instead of negotiating with the client directly. By enabling the competencies necessary to negotiate in both directions, you increase your revenue and your profit.

# The Character Traits That Enable Effectiveness

One of the challenges in increasing an individual's effectiveness is that sometimes they have the skills, but their character traits get in the way. For instance, in one company I noticed that some salespeople who were very good at prospecting didn't generate as many opportunities as salespeople who were not nearly as effective. The reason they didn't produce as many opportunities was because they didn't pick up the phone and dial the number of their prospective clients, instead relying on low-value and low-engagement vehicles like email. They didn't lack the skill to prospect; they lacked the self-discipline.

Here is a rather long list of competencies, each with a short explanation to help you recognize what prevents a salesperson from improving their results and their contributions to revenue growth.

## Personal Competencies for Effectiveness

- **Self-Discipline:** the ability to keep the commitments you make to yourself; the ability to will yourself to do what needs to be done without failure.
- **Optimism:** the ability to retain a positive, empowered attitude in the face of the challenges, obstacles, and losses that are part of professional sales.
- **Competitiveness:** the strong desire to win. Effectiveness stems from a salesperson's motivation to figure out how to win.
- **Resourcefulness:** the ability to figure things out on your own enables you to solve your own problems and address the obstacles that prevent your results.
- **Initiative:** people with initiative don't need to be told to do something because they are already taking care of it. The ability to be proactive is incredibly important to effectiveness, especially in sales.

- **Persistence:** the ability to keep working toward a certain outcome without giving up. The effectiveness here comes from the person's determination.
- **Accountability:** your prospective clients want to buy from someone accountable for the results they sold—and promised—them.
- **Focus:** more than ever, effectiveness comes from the ability to focus on one thing instead of being distracted by all the triggers in the modern work environment.
- **Confidence:** most highly effective people believe in themselves, creating the effectiveness that comes from knowing they are going to be able to achieve the results they need.
- **Courage:** salespeople have to be comfortable with the conflict that is sometimes present in sales.
- **Curiosity:** the desire to learn and make discoveries about how the world works. This creates effectiveness by being genuinely interested in understanding and helping their clients.
- **Passion:** the most effective people are passionate, giving themselves over to their work. Their intensity contributes to their effectiveness.
- **Success Orientation:** my favorite character trait for effectiveness, as hunger provides the motivation to succeed.

## People Skills for Effectiveness

- **Emotional Intelligence:** allows the person to be aware of their own emotional states, as well as recognizing these emotional states in others, including clients.
- **Caring:** in sales, caring is a superpower. It provides the salesperson with the ability to be other-oriented, creating a level of effectiveness that is unavailable to the self-oriented.
- **Street Smarts:** there is a certain advantage to being savvy: having the shrewdness and practical knowledge needed to make good decisions around people.

- **Reading People:** allows the salesperson to recognize and understand contacts' motivations and their needs.
- **Communication:** two communicative competencies lead to effectiveness—listening to understand and speaking in a way that ensures you are understood.
- **Authenticity:** effectiveness here comes from being who you are, being comfortable in your own skin. It's relatively easy to identify a fake or a fraud.
- **Sense of Humor:** this is less about telling jokes and more about the ability to engage and entertain your prospects.
- **Diplomacy:** the ability to resolve or prevent conflict. Because business comes with conflict, effective salespeople must work through issues and challenges.

This is a pretty complete look at an individual's potential competencies, whether they derive from internal character traits or the other-oriented traits that allow salespeople to win or lose deals. Use the list to identify the traits that are underdeveloped or missing altogether in your sales force. Coaching your team for growth should target their effectiveness. That may require enabling or boosting one or more of these traits, even if you think the person's doing a perfectly good job without it.

# PART

# IV

# An Eye to the Future

THE TWO PARTS of this book provided you, the growth leader, with strategies to prepare yourself to succeed in your role. As we moved forward, we turned to accountability and the structures that support it. From there, we shifted our focus to the individuals that make up your sale team, focusing on their effectiveness. Up to this point, accountability has mostly been about solving the problem of creating opportunities. Now we return to focus on winning the opportunities that generate revenue growth, including how to capture them and how to forecast them. Ultimately, this is what you are accountable for. If the pipeline makes up the arteries and veins of the sales organization, opportunities are the blood that provides the body with life.

# 11

## Opportunities

WE USE THE word *effectiveness* to describe the efficacy of an individual salesperson or a sales team. The more effective the individual, the easier it is to win opportunities. The less effective, the more difficult it will be for them to capture opportunities. There are a couple ways you might measure effectiveness. One is to look at a salesperson's win rate—a good metric, even if it doesn't always tell the whole story. A salesperson might have a great win rate in Q1 because they had good timing and good fortune, but it's unlikely they can ride that luck all the way through Q4. The second way you might measure effectiveness is the size of the client a salesperson is capable of winning, especially winning on their own. A combination of the two gives you a better picture of the individual's real sales effectiveness.

Your role as the leader is to teach, train, develop, and coach your team, improving their effectiveness in winning more than their "fair share" of the deals they pursue. In this chapter, we will look at the conversations that will help improve your team's effectiveness and help them win more deals.

## A Full Opportunity Review

When we discussed the Weekly Pipeline Meeting, I warned against using that time to talk through the status of each deal. The reason you can make the pipeline meeting a group event is because it is short and because it creates accountability. There is no value in your sales force listening to their peers talk about the status of their deals when they could be working on their own deals.

To supplement pipeline meetings, you need Full Opportunity Review (FOR) meetings, which are held individually. The cadence for these meetings should be based on your sales cycle, which determines how frequently you need to stay in touch with your team and how you keep up on your pipeline. A very short sales cycle may require a biweekly meeting, while a longer sales cycle might mean you review all the opportunities once a month. A super-long sales cycle, the kind where a deal takes more than a year to win, will still need a FOR meeting, even if it's only every two months.

The reason to review all of a salesperson's opportunities is to ensure they have enough opportunities, the right opportunities, deals of an appropriate size, and an overall healthy individual pipeline. Here are five problems you should pay special attention to in your FOR discussions.

1. **Too Few Deals.** It is not uncommon to see a pipeline with too few deals, even though the potential revenue is more than enough for the salesperson to reach their goal. When losing one of those deals would all but ensure they miss their goal, you can be certain their pipeline is fragile. By the time the main contact calls the rep to tell them "we decided to go another direction," it's often too late to recover.

2. **Too Small Deals.** Even after you coach your team's territory and account plans, you may discover that a salesperson has a reasonably large number of unreasonably small deals. There are a number of potential causes here, including poor targeting, a willingness to treat every deal as equal, or a lack of confidence. Your role in this case is to discern why the pipeline has so many small deals and what you need to do about it. The competency model in this book will help you with the second task, especially in terms of your salespeople's confidence.

3. **The Wrong Deals.** Here is where I embody the autocratic leader. There is no reason to allow a salesperson to spend time and energy on deals that you don't want. In one of my businesses, there is a minimum price that a client must pay or we will refuse their business. Revenue with no profit

is like empty calories; they offer no nutritional value for the sales organization. You want to remove these non-deals out of the pipeline as soon as you discover them, ensuring the salesperson knows what you *don't* want. Not all deals are created equal, and it's best to pursue the ones that are more equal.

4. **Deals All Bunched Up.** Even though we acknowledge that the sales conversation and the buyer's conversation are both now nonlinear, when you see deals all bunched up in one stage, you have reason to be concerned about your pipeline and the salesperson's lack of effectiveness. An opportunity review should reveal areas where the salesperson needs help. You want a conveyor belt for a pipeline, with everything consistently moving forward.

5. **Zombie Deals.** There is an old saying that time kills deals. That isn't exactly correct: time with no forward movement kills deals. As long as deals are progressing, all is well. If a salesperson's deal is old enough that they've had to renew their driver's license since the deal's last progress, it's a zombie. You don't have to stop the salesperson from pursuing that client, but you do have to move the deal back to target and have the salesperson start over.

All of these are problems of effectiveness. Having too few deals may arise from too little activity, but the inability to command a meeting is a pure effectiveness problem. Much of the time, having "too small" deals indicates the salesperson is not targeting the right clients, can't gain meetings, or lacks the confidence required of larger deals. A salesperson with bad deals is often using an approach that doesn't create enough value, finding it easier to move to lesser prospects. If you see a number of potential opportunities that are stuck, the salesperson is missing something they need to advance a sale.

## Deal Strategy: The Most Fun You Can Have at Work

If there is anything more interesting and more fun than deal strategy, it probably doesn't involve spreadsheets and conference tables. You'd never trade a deal strategy review for, say, drafting a new compensation plan or sitting through a forecasting meeting to update the numbers you just reported 24 hours earlier. But deal strategy, that's enough to cause your heart to speed up and your synapses to fire, as you prepare to help a salesperson or your entire team strategize their next win.

There is a certain type of client that generates what I call high-visibility, high-value, must-win deals. The high visibility means it's going to be on your senior leadership's whiteboard. It also means they are going to ask you about your progress more often than they should. But these opportunities are also visible to your competitors and the rest of your industry, meaning they'll know you've won even without a press release. These deals are valuable to you when it comes to revenue, profit, and reputation. They're also high-value for what will be your new client, because they will benefit tremendously by working with you.

Must-win, of course, means you must win it to meet your goals. Losing means hiring three grief counselors to help comfort the three or four senior leaders, who may well spend the next week rocking back and forth in the fetal position. Even when there are high stakes, formulating deal strategy is still one of the best parts of leading growth. Let's take a look at a few elements of deal strategy, including some factors that may or may not be on your linear sales process checklists.

### Is the Client Compelled to Change?

Whether your prospective client was already compelled to change or you compelled them to explore change and the better results they need, without understanding what is compelling the client to change, you will struggle to think through your deal strategy.

You want to go beyond the "presenting problem" and understand the root cause of their poor results.

**Questions**

- Why is this client compelled to change and what is driving this decision?
- What does the client want or need?

## *Who Is Leading the Client's Change Initiative?*

No matter how many stakeholders shuffle in and out of meetings, there are one or two people who are going to drive the process— and potentially, the decision. Knowing who the "centers of gravity" are in a deal allows you to understand what they want, why they want it, and whom you are going to need to support any change, including whom they choose as a partner.

**Questions**

- Which stakeholders are you working with now?
- How much effort are they putting into this initiative?

Note: client effort is a way to gauge the client's engagement and how serious they are about changing. It can also provide evidence about whether they have a preference to buy from you.

## *Which Leaders Can You Access?*

You may or may not have a leader engaged in the process, but when you don't, it's very difficult to determine your odds of winning a deal. Without knowing how this potential initiative scores on leadership's priorities, you have to be less certain about winning. Someone is going to have to sign a contract and a check.

## Questions

- Who is the senior leader who will need to green-light this initiative?
- Has that leader joined any meeting up to this point?
- How does this rank on their list of priorities?

### What Access Do You Have to the Organization?

As much as it pains me to say this, selling was easier when most companies just had a buying committee. Now you will most likely need organizational consensus, since 21st-century business functions are larger and more diverse. The larger the deal, the more important consensus will be.

## Questions

- Do we have access to the departments that are going to weigh in this initiative and our approach?
- How far behind are they in the conversation and what's our plan to catch them up?

### Whom Else Are They Considering?

It's nice when you know whom you are competing against, but your prospective client probably won't let you scan their guest-book for competing salespeople. There is nothing you can do to change your competitor's behaviors, but you can triangulate those behaviors by shredding their model (see my book *Elite Sales Strategies*).

## Questions

- What do you know about the competition?
- Have you had any feedback from your main contacts?

## *How Are We Differentiating?*

Differentiation is largely about creating a preference to buy from you. You should know how your salesperson has positioned themselves, your company, including how they've explained what makes your company different in a way that might provide you an advantage.

### Questions

- Is there anything that stands out as a competitive advantage?
- How does the client believe we are different?
- Do our differences make us a better fit than other options we know our competitors are going to use to position themselves?

A large part of deal strategy is ensuring the salesperson working a deal isn't making mistakes and unforced errors. To identify and prevent those errors, you may need to ask other questions to hone this part of your strategy. The more critical questions a salesperson *can't* answer about their potential deal, the less likely they are to win the opportunity.

## *How Do We Win?*

The money question here is how you intend to win the deal, but don't assume it's easy or even straightforward. As you build a plan to support your salesperson's pursuit, there are three primary factors you might want to consider.

1. **The Value of the Sales Conversation.** The first and perhaps the most important factor in winning deals is the value the salesperson creates inside the sales conversation. The reason your sales approach matters is that if your contacts are not benefiting from a conversation, it is unlikely they are going to prefer to buy from the salesperson or their company.

Any contact who believes your salesperson has taught them how best to make the decision they are charged with making will prefer to buy from that person, not least because their expertise provided confidence and certainty.

2. **Understanding the Client.** The better a salesperson understands the client and their business, the greater their chances of winning the deal. This is one reason tenured salespeople can improve in a vertical very rapidly. One factor that makes prospects hesitant to buy is that they don't believe the salesperson "understands their business." This indicates two problematic sales behaviors. First, it often means the salesperson didn't ask the right questions. Every client needs a salesperson to understand certain information before moving forward with them. It's often impossible for a salesperson to come to the sales conversation with this knowledge. It needs to be discussed during the sales conversation, and the only way to ensure that happens is to ask the right questions. Second, it may suggest the salesperson lacks business acumen, making them unable to connect the dots between the client's challenges and what they need to do to improve their results. Many clients' challenges are the result of larger, systemic, issues in their industry or environment.

3. **How You Deliver the Desired Outcomes.** Most sales organizations compete against other companies that are all capable of improving the client's results, some more effectively than others. Delivering those results is one way to differentiate yourself. The more you ensure your contacts feel that you have adjusted your approach to account for their preferences, the more stakeholders will prefer to buy from you.

Every deal has its own strategic nuances, but these three factors seem to be universal. Allow your professional intuition to guide you: if your gut tells you something feels wrong, take the time to explore it and go meet with the client yourself, if necessary. Net new revenue comes from winning opportunities. Missing your goals is the result of not winning enough of the opportunities that your team creates and pursues.

## How Could We Lose?

A lot of sales leaders like to ask how the salesperson intends to win without considering how they might lose. You want to ask both questions. No salesperson will argue (I hope) that they might lose because they don't create enough value, understand their client, or deliver the outcomes appropriately. Newer salespeople might worry that a higher price will cause the client to buy from a competitor, even though that is less likely than they believe. Here are four factors to explore instead:

1. **Who Prefers Us and Why?** I know we are supposed to believe that relationships don't matter, but they are incredibly important for winning new opportunities and new clients. If a salesperson doesn't know whether the decision-makers prefer them, that's a sign that their deal is in trouble. The salesperson's experience might tell them that the decision-maker prefers them to make statements that allow the salesperson to know how they're doing. The more evidence that people other than the decision-maker think the salesperson is doing well, the better.
2. **Client Time.** We track a lot of information in sales, especially activity. But we track very little when it comes to the sales conversation. It is easy to measure time, and when decision-makers provide a salesperson more time, that suggests they have some preference for that salesperson. The opposite is also true: the less time a prospect is willing to give a salesperson, the less likely they are going to capture the opportunity.
3. **Potential Dealbreakers.** In conversations with their contacts, the client's needs sometimes surface "dealbreakers,"

something nonnegotiable that the prospective client needs. An inability or unwillingness to provide certain results or deliver them in a certain way can cost the salesperson their potential deal and cost you your net new revenue. Maybe there are no dealbreakers, but it's worth tracking even potential ones. If you are not sure, ask the salesperson to ask their contacts.

4. **Competitive Threats.** There is nothing you can do to change your competitor's behaviors, so there isn't a lot of value in talking about them. There is, however, every reason to know how your competitors attempt to beat you for deals, so you can disrupt their competitive strategy. For example, a competitor that competes on price can be easily crushed by a salesperson who understands triangulation strategy— explaining to the client that some business models will require a certain set of unspoken concessions necessitated by the lower price, then showing how the client will not achieve their results without the right investment. (See my book *Elite Sales Strategies: A Guide to Being One-Up, Creating Value, and Becoming Truly Consultative* for more on triangulation strategy.)

The value of this approach is that the more you help your sales force improve their effectiveness, the greater their results. You want every salesperson on your team to become more effective over time; that's the primary idea behind pulling the bell curve sharply to the right (Chapter 10). You can train your sales force how to think about how they win deals by asking them questions. Any time a salesperson can answer all your questions without hesitation, ask them new questions that enable them to become even more effective at winning deals.

As leaders, we fail our salespeople if we don't help them become more effective while they are in our charge.

## The Two Reasons to Join a Salesperson on a Sales Call

There are two important reasons you should join a salesperson on a sales call. First, it is the only way to know how the salesperson performs in front of a client. Even though the salesperson may be uncomfortable with you sitting next to them the whole time but saying nothing, you will have a lot to talk about later. You can start this conversation by asking the salesperson how they believe the call went, giving you some understanding of how they judge their own performance. Unless the salesperson made an egregious mistake, you don't want to criticize them immediately. Instead, you want to note all the things they did well, then share with them what they might do better in the future.

The second reason to join a salesperson on a sales call is to contribute to the pursuit by engaging as an active participant. You can improve an important conversation by showing your interest in the client and their needs, as part of the leadership function of your company. The best way to handle this kind of sales call is to plan what areas you are each going to cover. For a must-win deal, you may need to see for yourself how you are tracking and what might need to change.

## Strategies for Sales Domination

In general, strategies seek to dominate your opponents, not just compete with them. Specifically, you can dominate three elements of the sales process: presence, time, and narrative. These three tactics for creating a competitive advantage are not always easy to employ, but encouraging your team to use them can help you win deals you might otherwise have lost.

## Dominating Presence

First off, there is an advantage created only through a physical presence. The salesperson who travels to see their prospective client is communicating something important to the client—without having to say a word. The fact that you traveled to their location means you care. Your salesperson's contacts will believe the salesperson knows more about their business than the salesperson who refused to show up or insisted on Zoom.

In March 2021, Jamie Dimon, the CEO of JP Morgan Chase, was interviewed on CNBC. Dimon explained he was canceling all of his videoconference meetings, but what followed was far more interesting and even more important. Dimon said that he and his team had spoken to all the clients they lost during the pandemic. The single reason they chose to buy from Dimon's competitors instead is because they showed up and Chase's salespeople did not.

## Dominating Time

Let's imagine that a large prospective client is going to meet with three sales organizations, an expensive and significant time commitment. Most sales organizations do their best to be polite and perhaps even servile, complying with the client's process—even if it doesn't serve the client's goals. A lot of salespeople believe that compliance can replace value creation, even though facilitating a bad decision will not improve the client's results. Fortunately, you know better than that. Use the time you have to show why working with you will benefit the client, even when that means teaching them a better way to make decisions.

Creating the advantage of time also means creating more and greater value than your competition. This is the reason you need a value-creating approach to sales, as well as the kind of advice most salespeople won't even attempt to offer their clients: advice about how to buy, what conversations your clients must have to make the best decision, and whom they need to include in the conversation and their decisions. There is an asymmetrical advantage that accrues to salespeople who can gain more of the client's time, with the aim of crowding out their competition. Even a couple of extra hours allows deeper, less transactional conversations. You want your team to play chess while your competitors are playing tic-tac-toe.

## Dominating the Narrative

This is a tactic that few are aware of, especially when they have a legacy approach to B2B sales. The narrative is your version of reality, including what is good and true. Sharing this narrative allows you to capture your contact's mindshare, influencing how they understand their world.

The salesperson who uses their presence and time to help their prospective client better understand their world and their reality provides something far different than their competitor's "why us" talk tracks. Explaining why and how the client should change, including how to weight different factors, scores points by providing the insights that come from the salesperson's expertise and experience.

Some sales forces believe their company's history, their clients, and their products and services form the only narrative they must deliver to their clients. Believing that talking about these subjects creates a preference is likely the root cause for their low win rates and most of their salespeople missing their goals.

## Winning Net New Revenue

Your win rate is one important way to judge your effectiveness in improving your team's effectiveness. To win more deals, you need to increase each individual's ability to create and win opportunities from their existing clients, as well as to gain the new logos that will create new revenue now and potential revenue in the future.

As you read this book, you are going to make a number of changes, some more difficult than others. This book offers a comprehensive approach to revenue growth, and it's easy to pick the easy changes while avoiding the difficult ones. In particular, you might be tempted to spend an inordinate amount of time on opportunities, especially because it is highly engaging and more interesting than a lot of other necessary changes.

Here's the truth: no matter how high your win rate, if you don't have enough opportunities, you are not going to create the revenue you need to reach your goals. If you don't deal with the decisions you need to make, instead of kicking the can down the road, you'll suffer with poorer results longer than necessary.

# 12

## Forecasts

MUCH OF THE time, your CRM will help you forecast deals about as effectively as tarot cards, a crystal ball, or the entrails of a chicken. You may have a better track record on your March Madness brackets than on trying to forecast your quarter. Predicting what people will do is never easy, which is why some sales leaders describe their pipelines as "pipe lies" that run on "hopium."

The only way you can confidently forecast your quarter is to win the deals you need before you forecast. Other than that, any deal without a signed contract has a 50-50 chance of being won. You can argue all you want about sales math, but I assure you there are only two outcomes: winning and losing.

## A Misunderstanding of Sales Math

When you install a CRM, let's say Salesforce.com, the preset percentages aligned with each stage of a deal suggest your likelihood of winning that opportunity. The first stage in Salesforce's template is titled "Prospecting" and it shows the percentage as 10 percent. Unless your team wins 10 out of every 100 records in your CRM, there is no evidence to suggest you have *any* chance of winning a prospect's business before you have ever communicated with them.

The second stage is "Qualification," which Salesforce also gives 10 percent odds of winning. Following this senseless logic, you have the same chance of winning a deal with qualified as with unqualified prospects—it claims that qualifying someone literally does nothing to improve your results. Just doing a "Needs Analysis" (stage three) allegedly doubles your chances of winning, even if the discovery call was awful and ended without a next step for your salesperson. Apparently, any meeting that you might call "Needs Analysis" gives you an automatic one-in-five chance.

The next stage is called "Value Proposition," which boosts your chances from 20 percent to 50 percent, even for doing little more than explaining how your "solution" is a good fit for your prospective client. The next stage is "Identifying the Decision-Makers," valued at 60 percent, even though you might be wondering why your sales force delivered the value proposition to anyone besides a decision-maker. I admit I don't know what the stage called "Perception Analysis" means, but it moves you to a 70 percent chance of winning. Just handing off a proposal and pricing increases your win rate by 5 additional points, giving you a three-in-four chance of winning. Negotiating makes it almost a sure thing, with a 90 percent chance of winning.

This approach is no better than guessing. Just consider a few common scenarios to see what I mean.

## Scenario 1

One of your best salespeople has completed the "perception analysis," and has updated the opportunity fields. The opportunity is now sitting at a very confident-looking 70 percent chance of crossing the finish line. But as you are working on a deal strategy to make sure your salesperson wins, she tells you that your company is one of three companies the client is considering. She's a great rep, though, so you are not worried.

The problem here is that the math literally does not add up. If your best salesperson has a 70 percent chance of winning the client's business, that means both your competitors are splitting a 30 percent chance of winning the same deal, giving each a 15 percent chance of winning—even though their CRM shows them the same 70 percent chance given their respective progress. If you are confused, let me make this simple: the CRM has split a 210 percent "probability" into thirds, making your actual odds of winning 33 percent—the exact chance you have to win a deal when you compete against two other companies.

## Scenario 2

Your new, highly experienced salesperson reports that they're in the final negotiation for a must-win deal—the almighty 90 percent level on your CRM. But before the negotiation begins, the client sends your new rep an email to ask for your best and final offer. The salesperson didn't know the promiscuous decision-maker was still engaged with other potential partners. Whatever happened to going steady?!

Because we have already done this exercise, you now know you have, at best, a 50-50 chance of winning the business. But you have a hunch that, because you also have the highest price, the competitor's "best and final offer" might reduce your chances to something closer to zero.

## Scenario 3

Your salesperson found a way into a very large company. It was a pleasant surprise when he managed to book the meeting, but you are also concerned about the salesperson's ability to handle an opportunity this big and complicated. Fortunately, the decision-maker seems to like the salesperson and wants to work with this salesperson specifically, something you are (silently) struggling to understand. The salesperson has already spent hours onsite with the client, and he soon reports that he is going to give the client a proposal and pricing, much sooner than you believed possible.

You assess the chances at something close to 20 percent, as that's been the salesperson's win rate at your company so far. And even adding up all those wins would barely reach a quarter of the value of this deal. There's no way this will work out for you, so you don't even bother to put this opportunity in your forecast. But it doesn't matter, because the salesperson returns to the office with a signed contract and the largest revenue deal of the year, one that will be difficult to beat by any segment of your bell curve (true story).

As it turns out, the decision-maker and the salesperson are both from the same small town in North Carolina, where all of the salesperson's people are practically kin with all of the decision-maker's people. Now why didn't Salesforce think of that?

## Generating Useful Sales Insights

There is strong tendency to treat sales like a science, even though it's more of a craft. Science is the pursuit of what is true. A scientist with a hypothesis tests their hunch by running an experiment. If the experiment proves the hunch to be correct, other scientists run the same experiment to verify or falsify the hypothesis. It's called replicating results, and it is possible because of the unchanging laws that govern our planet.

If sales were truly a science, it would be fully repeatable. For example, a green-eyed salesperson follows the exact steps outlined in your highly linear and super-prescriptive sales process and wins a client's business. Meanwhile, his blue-eyed colleague executes the same process and loses spectacularly. To hear some sales leaders talk about scientific sales forecasting, you'd have to conclude that the second client must hate people with blue eyes, probably because their junior-high crush went to the prom with that blue-eyed jerk from math class. All you have to do is update your Salesforce algorithm to account for lost loves, right?

Let me suggest a better way. First, look at the total deals each salesperson has won and divide it by the number of deals they pursued. That might tell you that Salesperson A won five out of ten deals, giving them a 50 percent win rate, a fine number. But as you look closer at the data, you notice they won the five smallish deals and lost all five of the larger revenue deals. This simple analysis can get you closer to being able to predict which deals will close and which are not going to add logos to your slide deck anytime soon.

You can glean additional insights from looking at how and where individuals have trouble in the sales process. Of Salesperson

A's five losses, four would-be clients dropped out after their second discovery call. While this does offer some idea of what to forecast and what to leave off your reports, it also helps you to recognize where that salesperson might need additional help.

If you really want to get granular about each individual on your team, you can do some more math, using individual success rates to make an educated guess about their pipelines. Let's assume Salesperson B pursues 20 prospective clients and wins 2 new clients.

- **Qualification:** 20 clients in this stage with two eventual wins means the salesperson has a 10 percent chance of winning a deal.
- **Discovery:** Because 8 prospects moved to this phase, the salesperson has a 25 percent of winning a deal (two divided by eight).
- **Needs Analysis:** The 7 clients that moved forward in the process indicate a 29 percent chance of winning.
- **Value Proposition:** The next three stages are all the same, with 6 contacts moving into the next stages, suggesting a 33 percent chance of winning a deal.
- **Decision-Makers:** 33 percent.
- **Perception Analysis:** 33 percent.
- **Proposal Price:** The four deals that made it all the way to a proposal mean the salesperson has a 50 percent chance of winning.
- **Negotiation:** Three negotiations and two wins for a total of 67 percent.

Go to www.thesalesblog.com/leadinggrowth to download a spreadsheet you can populate with your own data.

## The Barbell Strategy

Imagine a barbell: a long metal bar with equal weight attached to each side. The weight on one side represents an extremely conservative approach with reasonable, stable results and rewards, while the other side represents an extremely aggressive approach, one with tremendous risk and equally titanic rewards. Your pipeline might have several weights on the conservative side of the bar but far fewer on the risky side.

We have to be careful with the idea of weight in this metaphor. Balancing this barbell isn't about the size of the deals alone: small or medium deals are not always conservative, and large deals are not always risky. Instead, you are measuring the risk and reward, with the conservative side, including large deals that have less risk associated with them.

The more weight you have on the conservative side of your barbell, the greater your ability to pursue deals that, while longshots, will provide an enormous payoff should you win. What exposes you to harm is having too little on the conservative side and far too much on the risky side. For instance, you could have three large, low-risk deals on your conservative side and one very large deal on your high-risk side. You could also have a large number of medium-sized deals on the conservative side, plenty to make your goal, with a single monstrosity of a longshot on the high-risk side.

## Tracking Two Pipelines

The need for two (or maybe three) pipelines is not well-recognized by either sales leaders or salespeople, especially those who target large prospective clients in opportunities that take a long time to create and win. When your strategy is built on winning giant clients who spend significant money and consider what you sell to be "strategic" in nature, you can experience huge fluctuations in results.

To ensure that you are winning deals every quarter, you need a second pipeline, one that contributes the revenue that buys you the time to pursue your dream clients. Think of it this way:

your strategic pipeline includes the large, long-cycle, strategic clients you are pursuing for big paydays. The operational pipeline focuses on smaller, shorter-cycle clients that create significant, if not massive, revenue.

## Improving Your Forecast Accuracy

We tend to measure the time it takes us to win a deal by starting with the first meeting and ending with the day the client signs the contract. That's not a terrible way to measure cycle time, but it isn't quite accurate. Allow me to explain why another measurement provides a more accurate picture and demands a second pipeline.

A larger and more strategic target client is certain to have a partner who already provides them with what you sell. That means they have a contract in place, as well as deep partner relationships, some built over years, that have survived the challenges of executing many tasks for the client. Many of these prospective clients may not even consider changing partners for months or years, so both opportunity creation and opportunity capture will take significant time. We call this approach Year Zero, the idea being that the opportunity may not present itself until Year One or Year Two, or even Year Three.

Here's my point: you delude yourself when measuring sales cycle time if you remove the year—or years—you spent getting to the first meeting. One reason sales leaders and salespeople struggle to create consistent revenue growth is that the biggest opportunities in their pipeline have long cycles, ones often subject to fits and starts.

The best thing about pursuing very large prospective clients is that you can be certain that they care about what you sell (as evidenced by what they spend with your competitor) and that their investment is strategic enough that it's critical to have the right partner. The significance of winning these "dream clients" cannot be understated. That's exactly why your strategic pipeline needs the protection of your second, operational pipeline.

Why would you ever want to win a $100,000 client when you could win a $2,500,000 client instead? But you can easily do both, working on the long pursuit using a Year Zero approach while simultaneously pursuing smaller yet still important deals. The operational pipeline provides a steady number of new deals that generate revenue while you are pursuing gargantuan opportunities. You want to hit singles, doubles, and triples as you set up for a home run.

## Managing Multiple Pipelines

Not a lot happens from day to day or week to week when you are pursuing large clients. You might have an hour-long meeting with your contact, with an hour of preparation on the front end and another hour to follow up on whatever you promised them. The updates from a pipeline meeting will only take a few minutes, but as things heat up, you may need to spend more time working on your strategy and pursuing the opportunity.

One of the reasons sales organizations and salespeople have results that look like a sine wave is because they win a big client in one quarter, giving it all of their attention and focus, which creates a crater in the next quarter—the result of not working hard to create and pursue other opportunities. Revenue can look like a sine wave too, especially when the big deal you counted on winning disintegrates when your prospective client gets acquired by their largest competitor, the senior leader takes another job, or the stakeholders decide to give your competitor a chance to turn things around.

Because large deals generally take more time, use the time between meetings to create and win smaller deals, but not too small. The operational pipeline moves faster, since the decisions to change are less complex and they don't always require as much work to change partners. What you are trying to do is fill in the down part of your sine wave, especially if your income trends dangerously close to zero.

Long-sales-cycle deals and short-cycle deals are different enough that they need different management. Too few large deals can harm your results, while too few medium-sized deals can find you with less revenue than you might need. The middle way is to pursue both large deals and not-so-large deals, pursuing the maximum revenue and removing the feast-or-famine pattern that comes from pursuing only large deals.

## Forecast Factors

It is difficult to forecast deals. It's important to remember that you may be forgiven for a poor forecast, but you will not be given nearly as much grace for missing your targets, something senior leaders should recognize.

There are a lot of factors you might consider as you determine whether or not you should forecast an opportunity. Exploring these factors will help you get a little bit closer to an accurate forecast. Though no single factor should guarantee a deal a spot in your forecast, combining several will give you a better picture.

- **Compelled to Change.** There is no reason to forecast a deal unless the salesperson can tell you why the client needs to change. The greater the detail about the need to change and how the poor results are harming their prospective client's business, the more evidence the opportunity is real, even if it isn't yet won.
- **Committed to Change.** There are some sales conversations where a senior leader tells the salesperson they are committed to making the change they need. In *The Lost Art of*

*Closing,* I suggested that salespeople ask the client directly if they are committed to change. You don't want to go through the whole sales process only to find they were just exploring. A statement about the commitment to change is a positive for forecasting.

- **The Stakeholders.** Even though BANT (budget, authority, needs, and timeline) provides a horrible experience for a prospective client, your sales team needs to address qualification, starting with the stakeholders. There is little doubt they will have a sponsor or coach, but it is less certain if they will have an executive who is aware of and interested in the change initiative. You want to know who is going to greenlight a change initiative. Too few stakeholders may cause you to hold off on forecasting.
- **Willingness to Engage the Organization.** In small deals, a salesperson might not have any trouble accessing the people they need to win a deal. As deals get larger, there is reason to be concerned that the salesperson has not met with or encountered people outside the department that is leading the change initiative (it's critical to understand your deal is your client's change initiative). When you are reasonably certain a deal is going to touch different areas of the business, you may want to postpone a forecast until you are certain your rep has access to the organization.
- **Client Effort.** Perhaps the most underrated factor on this list. A contact that is doing the work to move the opportunity inside their company is evidence, sometimes very strong evidence, that the client is going to buy. The more the salesperson can recognize the client is working for them specifically, the more you should consider forecasting. The less a contact is pushing things forward, the less willing you should be to include it in your commitments.

- **Delivery Model Fit.** Because we have sold solutions for such a long time, many salespeople believe their solutions are superior to their competition, making it difficult for them to face the reality that sometimes their solution isn't a good fit. Here's an example: the prospective client is a low-priced provider in their industry, and because that is true, they need a partner who can help them lower their costs. Your solution is way better, but your delivery model is at odds with your client's business model. I would never forecast this deal, though I would be happy to be wrong.
- **The Buying Process.** When asked about the client's process, a salesperson who doesn't know what the client needs to be able to buy may not be positioned well to determine the client's timeline. Salespeople don't like asking these questions because it makes them sound self-oriented. Good language includes something like, "Can you share with me your process on initiatives like this in the past, so I can make certain you have what you need from me and my team?" It's difficult to forecast a deal without knowing what the buyer needs.
- **Client Implementation Date.** For some sales organizations, it's important to know by what date a client needs to start. I have friends in businesses where their clients need to execute by August or they literally can't onboard them. A client with a firm date is better than a client that is okay with September or equally happy to wait until January the following year. These are very difficult scenarios to predict, and you may want to leave them out of your forecast until something changes.
- **Verbal Commitment.** A verbal commitment isn't worth the paper it's written on. That said, a verbal commitment to a salesperson is evidence someone is at least interested in buying from them. You might want to know who gave that

commitment and if they have the support of their team. If it's a senior leader, it's easier to believe. If the speaker is lower in the hierarchy, though, it's time to dig deeper.

- **Competitors.** We've already touched on competitors when it comes to math. When the salesperson is one of three pursuing the client's business, you should not predict a win—particularly if you've struggled to beat competitors in similar situations. Fortunately, there are also areas where you are strong and more likely to win. When you have a large number of positive factors on your side, you may be safe to put the deal in your commitment.
- **Your Gut.** When in doubt, trust your gut. Sometimes you will be wrong, and other times you'll be right, just like everyone else charged with guessing which deals cross the line. Sometimes, a salesperson knows for certain they are going to win or lose a deal, often during the first discovery meeting. Occasionally they are wrong, but having sold, you have had the experience of walking out a first meeting feeling the thrill of victory. You also know that you can easily lose deals you should have won.

In the end, the deal makes it into the forecast or it doesn't. By doing the work in this book, you will increase your chances of meeting your targets because you are creating more than enough opportunities.

## Making the Forecast Your Own

One company I am familiar with decided to forecast every day. To execute this perfect and worthless exercise, each sales manager had to update their forecast each and every day. As you might imagine, not much changed from day to day, but this group was desperate to update the scoreboard, some days finding the numbers hadn't changed in three or four days. In the hours of time it took them to calculate and post those updates, they could have been working on winning those deals they were pretending to update. You are always better off playing (and winning) the game than trying to guess the final score, especially when it's only the end of the first quarter.

If there is one thing I could impart to you here, it's that your forecast is your own. It's an exercise you do to ensure you create net new revenue, and to give you the certainty that you can reach your goals. That said, in some industries, a forecast is necessary to ensure the organization has the resources it needs to take care of its clients. You want to do your best at forecasting, even if it is difficult.

Your forecast will also help you gain a sense of why deals don't move forward or why a salesperson might be struggling to improve their effectiveness and their win rate. The attempt to determine which deals you are going to win on time, which will miss their dates, and which you will lose can facilitate a conversation about the salesperson and sales force's effectiveness. The questions you might use to test deals before forecasting them likewise exposes where people on your team need greater help.

# 13

## Protecting the Sales Force

THERE ARE CASES and cultures where you'll need to create a protective bubble around your sales force—a sort of force field to keep them from being dragged into work that isn't sales-related. I'm not saying here that sales is more important than the rest of the organization. Departments should be interdependent, needing each other like a steering wheel needs an engine. Neither am I saying that your salespeople should not be team players. But part of your job as a sales leader is to shield them from tasks and projects that might prevent net new revenue.

Let me be direct: there are forces inside the four walls of your company that would blur the line between sales roles and, well, everything else. It's important to maintain role clarity if you are going to lead growth. But before we talk about role clarity, let's explore why some otherwise nice, friendly, well-adjusted professionals have no problem stealing talented salespeople for tasks well outside their role.

## Non-Sales Tasks and Unclear Roles

Non-sales problems tend to find their way to two different kinds of salespeople. The first category comprises the skilled problem-solvers, the ones who have the competency to solve the problem better and faster than another person. Who has the greatest competency when it comes to addressing a client issue? If you answered "operations," "accounting," or "legal," please stop teasing me. The salesperson who won the client is always going to be the first choice. We'll come back to that problem later on.

The second category is the willing procrastinator—the type of salesperson who gladly accepts off-role tasks so they can "look busy" without doing the hard work of selling, particularly prospecting. They may even be good at those tasks, probably because they've spent more time practicing them. Some people in this group would be much happier in an account manager or customer success role, even though their conflict-aversion may limit their effectiveness in those roles too.

Salespeople in the first group are competent and have good relationships with their prospects, making them the natural choice to deal with the problem, as no one wants to be responsible for losing a client. There may be times when this is necessary, even if the salesperson is miffed at having to snatch defeat from the jaws of victory. Those in the second group rarely need to be asked—they're always at the ready to do whatever the client needs, even if the responsibility belongs to someone in another department.

Before we continue down this path, let me help you ensure that everyone on your sales force is a team player—without being forced into doing work that doesn't belong to them. In *The Only Sales Guide You'll Ever Need*, you will find a chapter on accountability. The main idea in this chapter is that the salesperson sells the outcomes their client needs—and promises to deliver them. Creating and winning opportunities is the salesperson's primary function. However, once the salesperson fulfills that function, the rest of the organization does the work that produces the promised outcomes.

To be team players without changing roles, your team will need to establish and maintain role clarity. Let's start by looking at some of the most common things salespeople are asked to do—even though these tasks clearly lie outside sales.

## Operational Tasks and Role Clarity

Say your salesperson receives a call from one of their clients. The client is missing an important shipment, and they ask the salesperson to help them find it. The salesperson wants to take care of their client, so they speed into action, trying to solve the mystery of the missing shipment. After sinking an hour into their search, the salesperson finally "gives up" and engages the operations team, who easily locates the shipment. The salesperson then calls their client to update them on their shipment and how the ops team saved the day.

If that sounds reasonable to you, you may have trouble reaching your net new revenue goal. It's nowhere close to reasonable. Here are the exact steps the salesperson should have taken:

1. **Salesperson Takes the Call.** There is no reason for a salesperson to avoid a call from their clients—including clients with a problem. You want your salespeople to take care of your clients, as that is part of the relationship. But instead of promising to find the shipment themselves, the salesperson tells the client they will call their operations team and have them call the client to locate the lost shipment.
2. **Salesperson Calls Their Operations Team.** The salesperson hangs up with their client and immediately calls their ops team, telling them about the client's problem. They then ask their colleague in operations to call the client to let them know they are working on finding the missing shipment. As a bonus, this introduces their client to a person who can help them in the future, preventing the client from having to play phone tag every time.
3. **Operations Reports to the Salesperson.** Because the salesperson was the first person to touch the problem, they need the operations rep to update them on the issue. Whether it's good news or bad news, the salesperson will need to follow up with the client since they have the strongest relationship.
4. **Salesperson Follows up with the Client.** Once the problem is solved, the salesperson calls their client and closes the loop. They also pass along the operation employee's phone number, in case the client has a similar problem in the future. You don't want a client with a serious problem to have to wait 90 minutes until your salesperson is done with another call or meeting, particularly when another employee could solve the problem in half that time.

Here is another common scenario to show the value of role clarity. Your client emails your salesperson with an accounting problem: the invoice they received is incorrect, so their accounts payable department won't pay it. The salesperson goes into the system, finds the incorrect invoice, and prints it out. But because there is no way to correct it without permissions to edit, he spends a little over two hours recreating a perfect replica in Microsoft Excel. He then uploads the template to the sales force's Slack channel, and pretty soon, three more salespeople have "corrected" their client's invoices.

There are two problems here. First, there is never a reason for a salesperson to retype or edit an invoice. That's just a waste of time. Second, by interfering with the accounts receivable department's duties, he can easily make things worse, especially once an unauthorized template starts making the rounds. Obviously, the call here would go to accounts receivable rather than operations, but the four-step process described above is the right way to avoid both problems and satisfy the client.

## Don't Demote Strategic Salespeople

To execute an effective modern sales approach, a salesperson must appear to be their client's peer. They need to be in a position of authority when it comes to helping their clients improve their results. As I've argued in *Eat Their Lunch: Winning Customers Away from Your Competition*, your salespeople need to create strategic value for their clients, the highest of the four levels of value. When you allow a salesperson to do work that belongs to other departments inside your company, even if it's their own idea, you are demoting them from a trusted peer to something much less. You also destroy their One-Up position with their client (see *Elite Sales Strategies*).

You may have to protect your salesperson from demoting themselves and lowering their stature. Nothing good comes from a salesperson who is not an equal with their prospective client, and even the appearance of subordination will harm their relationship. You should never allow a salesperson to do work that belongs to the other functions of your company. You should, however, have them engage in the strategic challenges their clients have, especially when they can help turn things around. The salesperson who hides from problems won't keep their clients very long.

## Operational Problems and Hostage Situations

When I was young and starting in sales, I did all kinds of things for clients, especially the really large clients that were vital to my company's livelihood. I'd hang time clocks on their walls, create reports, and in one case, I built a custom software program for them using Microsoft Access. I was competent enough to do all kinds of non-sales tasks and projects, and it felt nice to be needed. But feeling nice did nothing to increase my revenue. Eventually, I got the message and gave up anything outside of sales so I could spend my time and talent pursuing big deals.

Because salespeople are generally competent when it comes to client conversations, they are often asked to intervene and take care of the client's problem, challenge, complaint, or whatnot. Many—if not most—sales managers allow the operations team to poach a salesperson for a mission or two without saying a word. That's an expensive trade for sales, and colleagues— let alone clients—rarely pay them back in kind. The more you allow your finite resources to create outcomes that are not net new revenue, the less net new revenue you are going to produce.

When a salesperson gets dragged into something more than being a team player, go to the head of the department that kidnapped your salesperson and tell them you are now short a salesperson—and that you need them to send you someone to make cold calls and schedule meetings in that salesperson's place.

If it helps, remind them that Attila the Hun would leave one of his sons with his conquered enemies, taking one of their own sons home with him. It helped to keep the peace. Please smile when you ask the head of accounting to provide you with one of their introverted, compliant, and conflict-averse bean counters to book a meeting while your team retypes their invoices. Remind them that you need your entire team to reach your goals, just like they need all their spreadsheet jockeys to do their work. Promise the poacher you won't poach any of their team if they don't poach yours.

## Reps That Step to the Left

There is a dangerous trend in sales, one making it more difficult for sales leaders to reach their goals. Some salespeople (at least according to their business cards) decide to step to the left, abandoning their assigned role and adopting a new one. Overlook this practice at your peril—you will quickly find yourself short of your goals and struggling to make up for lost time and missing opportunities.

The account executive loves their big clients and their grandiose commission checks. What they don't love is having to prospect, creating new opportunities, and all the hassle of having to win new business. Why do all that work when you are already happy and financially comfortable? So the account executive keeps the title but begins to act like an account manager, doing all the non-sales tasks that keep them busy and their big clients happy: following up orders, generating reports, typing invoices, helping the client perfect their conference room feng shui, picking up quad vanilla mocha lattes for the client's entire team, and of course picking little Jimmy up from school and dropping him off at soccer practice. Before long, no one is quite sure whether he works for you or your client—and who could blame them?

There are some salespeople who prefer to be account managers. If one of them is taking up space on your sales team, the best decision is to move them into the role they want to occupy. With very few exceptions, salespeople who prefer the duties of an account manager have little trouble with the reduced compensation. It may be better to have a great account manager than to have a salesperson who no longer wants to create and win new opportunities. It's no fun, and mostly an exercise in futility, to try to shoehorn the account executive back into their role as a salesperson.

## Protecting Your Team from Pipeline Whiplash

There are other areas where you need to protect your sales team. Let's say you have had your collective heads down building a killer pipeline, one that is going to carry you and your team over the line. You and a couple of folks from your team are already daydreaming about the President's Club and a trip to the Cayman Islands. This will be your first time swimming with stingrays. Unfortunately, some stings hit closer to home: the people upstairs decide to change your company's priorities, launching a new product that now commands the whole sales force's time and effort. The company needs you to build a new pipeline, even though there are existing prospects who are deep into the sales conversation and who will buy in the next 60 days.

Even though it's no fun to argue with the suits and the spreadsheet jockeys, you have to do your very best to convince them to honor any and all deals that can be closed in the next 90 days. There are a number of problems you need to address, starting with the net new revenue these deals are going to create for you, your team, and your company. You have prospective clients who are counting on your team helping improve their results, and it's not fair to abandon them. It's also unfair that the salespeople compensated by commission will be harmed by the change of direction, both financially and reputationally. No matter how important the new initiative is, you are well within your rights to argue for a grace period, so your sales force can close out as much of their pipeline as they can.

There are some industries where leaders have no choice but to shift from one pipeline to another because of the way their business works. It is difficult for their sales forces to adjust, but in some cases, it's necessary. If that's true for you, you can best protect your sales force by ensuring they are agile enough to adjust to the reality of the business and what it needs. But even then, you must still fight for the chance to close the deals you can while you begin building another pipeline.

Expect some whiplash, by the way. In fact, as soon as the new product is launched, don't be surprised if Dear Leader and fellow executives ask you to go back to building your original pipeline.

## Beware Outsider Advice

Certain non-salespeople always think they have something to contribute to how salespeople should sell. You will find these people in your company, and you will occasionally see them pop up on LinkedIn to explain why they don't buy from salespeople— often saying they decide whom they want to meet with and reject anyone who uses cold outreach to pursue a meeting. They are only exceeded in annoyance by the vice presidents of sales who post about how they don't take cold calls (even as they insist their own salespeople make them), a performative contradiction bound to elicit a thunderbolt from the Gods of Sales.

Recently, for instance, I had a conversation with a marketing expert. I was explaining that some salespeople don't know the difference between a lead, a prospect, and an opportunity. I shared that a lead is nothing more than a name, a phone number, and an email address; a prospect is someone who may benefit from what you sell; and an opportunity is a prospect who is engaged in a conversation around change. My marketing expert claimed those distinctions were "why sales and marketing can't communicate," even though they are both responsible for creating revenue, but that isn't the biggest reason for the chasm between them.

What follows isn't very nice, and it isn't going to win me (or you) any popularity contests with the marketing folks. But it's the truth: with very few exceptions, most marketers do not spend time with prospective clients. Many wouldn't be able to point at your company's largest and most profitable client if they saw them in a police station lineup. Yet the marketing department is dead set on ruining sales calls by making salespeople answer "why us," a question that clients simply aren't asking. Normally, they waste 8 to 12 slides and 20 minutes on this question, an approach we can describe as a "terrible first date."

The poor, long-suffering decision-maker who hoped your sales-person might help them improve their results is first required to live through what amounts to a filibuster. Should you be required to use this approach on a first sales call, you have my permission to lie and suggest that your team is following the program to the letter. By actually helping your clients instead, you are no doubt saving lives—and deals. Those 8 to 12 slides can be transferred to the very end of the presentation, as a way to explain the resources your company will provide to ensure the client succeeds.

Marketing can play an important role for the sales function, but typically they are not yet aware that sales calls must answer the question "why change?" You can improve interdepartmental relationships—and your results—if you ask marketing to develop this content for you.

## Product Pushers and Their Promises

There is another group that, because they are not marketing, find themselves in the second slot in the slide deck. Call them civilians, muggles, or simply product leaders. These well-meaning people likewise believe they have something to contribute to sales, and they never fail to get time at the sales kickoff to train the sales force on the new product's "killer" features and benefits—because how else will you beat any and every product your competitors sell? At some point, they are contractually obligated to blurt out, "This product sells itself!" Reading Walter Isaacson's biography on Steve Jobs isn't enough to create demand. Whenever I visit a client site, I always wonder why I am able to walk straight through the front door, unmolested by the throng of potential clients chanting "shut up and take my money!"

You will never have to convince me that your product or solution is the very best in the category. I'll take your word for it. But I also believe your competitor's product or solution is the very best in the same category they share with you. As much as I wish your product or your solution had the instant mass appeal of the iPhone, I have yet to see such a product.

At the sales kickoff, the head of product teaches the sales force how to demo the product, making sure to share every feature, every benefit, and every advantage. They also learn how to differentiate the product from the competitor's incredibly similar new product. The good news is that yours is manufactured using ionized aluminum and your competitor's is made with stainless steel, making it weigh almost nine ounces more than yours. Naval Ravikant tweets, "You're doing sales because you failed at marketing. You're doing marketing because you failed at product." That hurts. But it doesn't hurt you or me or our sisters and brothers in sales. We are the failsafe when it comes to bad advice.

Most bad sales advice comes from people who've never actually tried it, especially not in a sales role. They're entitled to their opinions, and you're entitled to ignore every word.

## Tasks, Project Teams, and Feel-Good Initiatives

Often, role clarity comes down to where you allow your sales force to spend their time. Any time that is spent on nonrevenue tasks is time that would have been better spent creating and pursuing new opportunities. We've covered a great deal of the otherwise useful tasks that belong to others, but there are other threats, and the larger your company, the more the distractions.

Say a number of senior leaders want to build a task force to study the company's employee engagement. They want representation from every department, including sales. They ask you to provide two salespeople to help with this incredibly important project. The project will only take a couple of weeks, they insist, and it will be good for everyone going forward. It seems such a little thing, until you view it through the lens of revenue growth.

Missing two salespeople for two weeks means losing six new opportunities and the three deals they need to win to stay on course and reach their goals. There isn't any way to make up that ground, and even if some other salesperson adds three more deals during those "couple of weeks," it still deprived you of the deals you need. The question is, "Is it more important to generate the net new revenue we committed to or to scale back our goals to handle this other project?" Even if that sounds a little blunt, you are not likely to be praised for being such a good team player when you miss your sales targets.

Protect your team from CRM projects, new software presentations, or piloting one thing or another. They're on a mission. Your mission.

## Protecting Your Sales Force from Drama and Intrigue

Occasionally, the threat will be drama and intrigue. A senior leader leaves the company unexpectedly, and no one knows what happened or who is stepping into their role. The company has a very public problem that is covered by all the news channels, harming its reputation. The company's stock price plummets, making it a target for a hostile takeover. There is nothing you or your sales force can do about any of these things. Protecting your sales force requires you to address the facts or rumors, set them aside, and get back to the business of selling.

Finally, you will need to protect your team from the rest of the organization, including their failures. When your operations team is behind on production and is running late on their commitments, your team may have to do some damage control. Especially in that precarious situation, salespeople will worry about failing their clients while being asked to continue to acquire new opportunities. Protecting your team here means prioritizing clients for the operations team, to ensure that the must-keep clients get their shipments on time.

The worst thing you can do as a sales leader is allow your team to stop selling. It is incredibly difficult to regain that lost momentum, not just because of entropy but because in a quarter or two, when everything is back to normal, you are going to be missing the deals you should be closing. No one will remember why the sales team stopped selling, nor will they forgive you.

Heed well the boxing referee's advice: protect your sales force at all times.

# 14

## Cadence

A CADENCE IS an operating tempo. Much like in a musical performance, it outlines what a sales leader needs do to reach their goals by ensuring that individual salespeople hit their targets. With a cadence in place, you will have a much easier time handling one of the most difficult roles in business: sales management.

Unless you've had a sales manager that used a cadence, you may not have any idea what to do, when to do it, and how to manage your own work. The salesperson who finds themselves promoted into a sales management role often finds the work to be so different from what they know that they decide to keep the title but keep selling. These managers spend much of their day running around trying to close deals, something consultant Neil Rackham described as "buying a dog and barking yourself."

Your cadence allows you to build a calendar of events that ensures you stay on track throughout your sales year. Like all disciplines, it prevents you from being reactive and running from fire to fire, a practice that makes it impossible to do the proactive work that will improve your growth rate. Whether you call it a cadence or an operating tempo, the more you work in a disciplined, focused way, the better your results—and your team's results.

Some of the pieces of your new cadence will be familiar from Chapter 8. However, here we will spend more time exploring how to get everything onto a calendar. Our goal is to create a sense of control and perspective about what you and your team must do to succeed in creating growth. There is no one cadence that serves every sales leader equally well. Different companies and different sales leaders will need more or less of each element, so part of your task is to make your cadence your own.

Many of the design decisions will depend on the number of salespeople on your team and your average sales cycle. As you look at the long list of components that make up an effective cadence, don't worry about trying to design a perfect one. Seek instead to figure out what is good enough, as you can always make changes in the future.

## Introducing Your Annual Theme

The beginning of your sales year should start by clarifying your vision, your theme for the year, and what you are going to accomplish. Strong direction on what you and your team are going to accomplish can set everyone's direction for the year. This is a great time to share your new vision and the next phase of your transformation. Maybe you need to grow revenue and improve your profitability. You might also decide that you are going to pursue new deals in a vertical you haven't paid enough attention to in the past. You might make this "the year of displacement," with a focus on taking large clients from your competitors. And you'll never hear me complain about theming a year around improving sales effectiveness, something you can insist on by adding development to your cadence.

By theming your year, you can start to address areas that need improvement or focus on some area that will lead to greater growth and success. Even though you only need to do this once a year, you want to have your theme, your vision, and your goals designed before the year starts. Your first meeting of the year needs to provide direction for the next four quarters.

Provided you succeed in reaching your goals, you can change themes the following year, but only if you produced the results you committed to at the beginning of the year. I once spoke to a sales organization three years in a row. The first year I was with them, they decided to be "Challengers." The next year they decided to get "Back to Basics." The third year found this group focusing on "Better Questions." These aren't bad themes, but the company never did the work their annual theme required of them. Instead, the sales force learned that it was all kabuki: they were not going to be held accountable for whatever change the senior leadership brought out at the sales kickoff meeting, even though there was great fanfare and a sincere intention to adopt each theme. Every year, the theme was forgotten as soon as the sales reps jumped into their Ubers and headed to the airport. To make your theme stick, you want to create your new communication plan.

## Territory and Account Plans

We introduced this structure of accountability earlier in the book, and you may already be employing it. This is one of the areas where you will need to decide how often you need your team to update their plan, one you can help coach them through.

In a relatively long sales cycle, a B2B salesperson can update their territory and account plan every 90 days. Even though a lot of sales organizations employ a 90-day cadence, it isn't right for every team. One industry I am familiar with wouldn't need to update their territory and account plan more often than twice a year if that. They have incredibly long sales cycles, taking years to win a deal. Other industries with incredibly fast sales cycles might require a 60-day territory and account plan. Anything faster than that may not be worth your team's time.

Let me remind you here of a serious and significant threat, one that is difficult to reverse and that will cost you years without revenue growth. Companies with marketing that results in new leads for the sales force can lapse into a situation where the sales team stops prospecting, becoming dependent on marketing for leads. Over time, as the leads slow down, the sales force becomes less and less willing to do the work themselves, preferring to sit and wait for the next thimble of increasingly sparse lead data. It might be faster and easier to release the whole sales force, burn down your office building, and start over from scratch.

No matter how or why your sales force is busy, never, ever, allow them to stop prospecting. It would be easier to colonize Mars than to get a team that has not had to prospect to start prospecting again. Insist on a territory and account plan and hold your team accountable for executing it—even if they have incoming leads and opportunities. You could even use those leads as rewards for creating new opportunities, passing them out to the salespeople who are already winning targeted accounts in their territory.

Feed your hunters. Starve those who refuse to hunt. If this doesn't sound fair, please allow me to explain. There is never a reason to reward a person who is not doing the work required of them. When you decide to be "fair" in distributing leads, know that you are rewarding bad behavior, bad results, or both. The best way to help a salesperson with a detrimental reliance on leads is to remove their crutch and insist they prospect for new business.

## The Weekly Pipeline Meeting

Even if you started holding weekly pipeline meetings after you read Chapter 8 ("Structures of Accountability"), there is more to understand here. There are 52 weeks in a year. This means that a salesperson has 50 weeks or fewer to reach their goals. Let's look at some math to understand how and why sales managers miss their numbers.

For the sake of illustration, we're going to use very simple numbers here. The salesperson has a target of $1 million annually. They have a 40 percent win rate and an average deal size of $50 thousand. They thus need to win 20 deals to reach their goal. While the math is easy enough to understand, meeting these numbers is difficult under the best of circumstances, and will soon become impossible should the salesperson find themselves with no new opportunities each week.

Each of the 50 weeks the salesperson works, they need to generate a $50 thousand opportunity. Because they win at 40 percent, they are going to win a little over 1.6 deals, while losing 2.4 deals. But let's say this salesperson didn't create four opportunities in the first month of the year. Instead, they looked at their pipeline and decided it was good enough that they had no need to prospect. Because they didn't prospect, they created no new opportunities.

I understand how upsetting this scenario must be to you. Remember, it's just a hypothetical (until it isn't), but the time for you to be upset that your salesperson didn't create opportunities is at the end of the first week, not the end of the month—or the quarter. When sales leaders allow a salesperson to avoid addressing the fact that they didn't create the opportunities they needed for an entire month, there is no way to recover from the loss, at least not until you figure out time travel.

A weekly pipeline meeting is a good guardrail. It will prevent your team from harming themselves by believing they can make up for lost time. I would work very hard to avoid allowing more than a week to pass before ensuring your team has created the opportunities they need.

## Opportunity Reviews

This is another area where you will be required to determine the tempo of your meetings. The variables here include the number of salespeople on your team, as well as the average number of deals they have in their pipelines. A sales manager with eight salespeople can very easily review their team's opportunities every two weeks by meeting with half the sales force in one week and the other half the following week. Or by doing two reviews a day for a week, freeing up time for other tasks and obligations in the off weeks.

Opportunity reviews take time, making it incredibly difficult for a sales manager with 15 salespeople to carve out the time necessary to meet with each salesperson every two weeks. Without reviewing opportunities frequently enough, it is difficult to assess if a salesperson's deals are moving forward and to ensure the salesperson has a good strategy for each of their deals.

The other variable you need to consider is the number of deals each salesperson is pursuing. In industries where each salesperson is managing a lot of deals at one time, it may not be possible (or necessary) to review every opportunity. Instead, you might look at the salesperson's largest opportunities, using some opportunities as examples and asking the salesperson to apply the same deal strategy to similar deals.

It is much easier to review opportunities in longer sales cycles, where there tend to be fewer deals and more time to work on deal strategy. Opportunity reviews help you recognize the different effectiveness challenges of the individuals on your team, especially when their opportunities illuminate a problem like deals stalling in the same part of the sales conversation. This also allows you to assess deals to ensure they are progressing, troubleshooting them when necessary.

It's best if you get a look at the total opportunities every two weeks, but you are going to have to build your cadence around the number of reps, the number of deals, and your average sales cycle.

## Coaching Client Meetings

There are two different ways to coach client meetings. The first way is to review the salesperson's plan for their meeting. The second, and more effective way, is to accompany the salesperson on a client meeting.

When revenue growth is your goal, you must make sure the individuals on your team are prepared for big client meetings—meaning, they are ready to create value for their prospective client. Effective sales organizations don't take important meetings lightly. Instead, they prepare. You can coach the salesperson by having them describe the outcomes they intend to create for the client, as well as what next step they believe they need to acquire to move the opportunity forward. What's most important is creating value that would differentiate the salesperson and create a preference to buy from them.

One sales manager told me that he'd never met a particular salesperson on his team face to face, so he wasn't sure how to help him. Sure enough, he wasn't very effective in helping him improve his results. He had a lot of theories but, having never watched or listened to the salesperson talk to a client, he couldn't know what he needed to do to improve the salesperson's results. This problem often arises when your salespeople live and work in their own territory, because it's difficult to assess someone's performance from thousands of miles away.

The alternative to coaching is to get into the field with each individual salesperson as part of your cadence. You are not likely to find anyone else suggesting so drastic a step, but leading growth (and *Leading Growth*) is about creating and winning new opportunities. There is no better way to learn how to help your salesperson improve than joining them on a sales call. Watching the salesperson's approach on a discovery call will give you the clearest lens through which to judge their performance and their effectiveness. If you must travel to observe the individuals on your team, have them do their best to schedule you on a few different calls. Even if you only observe one sales meeting, though, it's worth your time. Beyond the meeting, you'll get a chance to spend time with the salesperson at lunch or dinner, giving you some idea about how best to help them succeed while also creating a better relationship.

## Coaching Personal and Professional Development

Part of a good and effective cadence is coaching the individuals on your team to enhance their personal and professional development. Research suggests that a lot of salespeople are interested in their own growth and development, so this practice is likely important to many of your team members. How you coach, of course, is going to depend on the individual.

When you coach experienced, successful salespeople, you want to use a nondirective approach. For instance, ask them what they would like to work on during your coaching session, then function mainly as a sounding board, asking them questions and challenging them when necessary. These conversations are designed to explore the new beliefs and new actions that may improve their already good performance. You can trust an experienced person to be able to do the largest part of the work once you provide prompts that let them explore their choices. The more mature, confident, and competent the salesperson, the more comfortable they will be when it comes to making change.

Coaching a relatively new salesperson—the kind who lacks the experience that would provide them the confidence and the competence to work independently—will require a different approach. It isn't helpful to ask a new salesperson what they need to work on and how they should go about making change. The greener the salesperson, the more your coaching is going to resemble training, with you explaining a concept, teaching them how to think about it, and giving them instructions on how to approach some outcome they need. You still need to ask them what they are going to do differently and when they are going to review their results. That type of reflection will help them understand why what they did worked or why it didn't work as well as they wanted.

You don't need more than a half-hour session to coach a salesperson. More is not better than doing it well, and a half hour of focus is enough to provide a salesperson with the ability to try something new. Remember, coaching is about behavioral changes.

## Coaching Time Management

One of the variables when it comes to revenue growth is the time the salesperson spends on sales-related tasks and outcomes. Some research suggests that salespeople spend only 34 percent of their time on sales-related tasks. And in a finding that should shock exactly no one, many salespeople improve their results simply by spending more time selling. Who would have guessed?!

You want to look at a salesperson's calendar, exploring what they would need to do to make more time for their two most important tasks. Say it with me: opportunity creation and opportunity capture are the keys to revenue growth. Feel free to use a regular coaching session for this topic, especially if you recognize that a salesperson needs to get control of their calendar or lacks the discipline that would improve their activity.

## Sales Training and Development

You are not going to find this in anyone else's advice on building a cadence. Most sales organizations, sales enablement, revenue teams, and sales trainers aren't concerned nearly enough about sales effectiveness. The problem with most sales organizations' training is that it only "checks the box," providing a day of info-dump training, often on something other than effectiveness.

There is no end of resources you can use to provide 20 minutes of developmental content to your sales team. Leading your team in a conversation about what they are going to do with the content, then following up to share results, can help everyone improve over time. You want to treat development as a long-term process, one that everyone should embrace, because the greater their effectiveness, the better their results.

One way to do this efficiently is to have a conference call late in the afternoon, to let people share with each other. You can also use that slot for a salesperson to talk through a deal, share their strategy, and answer questions from their peers.

## The Right Cadence

While it's difficult to do everything you need to do in a week, creating a sequence that works for you will provide you with the time you need to check all the boxes above. You don't need to do all these things in a week—just as often as you need to—and outside of pipeline meetings, many of them work just as well biweekly or even monthly (see Figure 14.1).

| january | | | | | 2022 |
|---------|---|---|---|---|-------|
| MONDAY | TUESDAY | WEDNESDAY | THURSDAY | FRIDAY | SAT/SUN |
| 27 December Click to add text | 28 Click to add text | 29 Click to add text | 30 Click to add text | 31 Click to add text | 1/2 January Click to add text |
| 3 Annual Theme and Plan | 4 Territory and Account Plans | 5 Territory and Account Plans | 6 Territory and Account Plans | 7 Territory and Account Plans | 8/9 Click to add text |
| 10 Pipeline Meeting | 11 Opportunity Reviews | 12 Opportunity Reviews | 13 Opportunity Reviews Sales Training | 14 Opportunity Reviews | 15/16 Click to add text |
| 17 Pipeline Meeting | 18 Coaching | 19 Coaching | 20 Coaching Sales Training | 21 Coaching | 22/23 Click to add text |
| 24 Pipeline Meeting | 25 Opportunity Reviews | 26 Opportunity Reviews | 27 Opportunity Reviews Sales Training | 28 Opportunity Reviews | 29/30 Click to add text |
| 31 Pipeline Meeting | 1 February Coaching | 2 Coaching | 3 Coaching Sales Training | 4 Coaching | 5/6 Click to add text |

Figure 14.1

Let's look at a cadence.

**January 1:** Yearly Theme and Plan (90 minutes)

**January 2:** Territory and Account Plan Review (60 minutes per salesperson)

**Weekly:** Pipeline Meeting (30 minutes each Monday)

**Bi-Weekly:** Opportunity Reviews (60 minutes per salesperson)

**Ad Hoc:** Coaching Client Meetings (as needed to ensure high-visibility, high-value, must-win deals are effectively pursued)

**Bi-Weekly:** Coaching (30 minutes per salesperson opposite to their opportunity review, adding time management when necessary)

**Weekly Sales Training:** (25 minutes of training or salesperson-led opportunity review)

There is no one-size-fits-all cadence; there are too many variables to consider. But not having a cadence is unacceptable. One of the choices you must make as a sales manager is whether you are going to devote more time and attention to working inside your company or to taking care of your sales force. A lot of sales managers like to spend time with their sales leader, partly so they can advance their own careers. Even though there is nothing wrong with pursuing more responsibility, if a manager isn't spending time with their team, no one is going to expect their future managers to do what they did.

# 15

## Your Next Vision

THE HIGHER YOU climb, the further you can see. From your new vantage point, what was once out of view comes into focus, providing you with a new vision. When you were still on the ground, you might have worried about net new revenue and your growth rate. You may have started with a conservative vision, a modest goal, and a growth rate you believed you and your team could accomplish without too much difficulty.

You will be elated to reach your goal, and deservedly so. Take a moment to be proud of yourself and your team. But when that moment passes, you'll be struck by the idea that you set your goal too low, your vision too limited. Had you been a little bolder, you'll realize, you would have increased net new revenue by some larger percentage and smashed your targets by an even greater amount. You'll also recognize what you need to change to do even better in the future. This is the beginning of your next vision.

## Assessing Your Activities

There are two primary variables to success in sales: activity and effectiveness. When you look at your results and the work you and your team must do to bring your new vision to life, the changes you need to make are almost certain to fall into one of these categories. My goal here is to convince you that "more activity" is not the only strategy available or necessary for growth.

You may need to increase your current activities, but you may also need to pursue a number of new and different activities, especially to keep boosting your net new revenue and your annual growth rate. It's naive to believe that you just have to ask your team to make more calls and book more meetings, especially when you have other activities that yield better results. In other words, new activities can increase effectiveness.

For example, you could keep your current level of prospecting but also create industry vertical specialists, directing the sales force's time and effort for the prospective clients who would benefit from working with a salesperson who understands their business. You are reallocating their activity. When this strategy is right for a sales organization, it can also increase effectiveness, because you are giving the client a subject-matter expert.

Changing some activities inside the sales conversation can also generate improvement. For example, you could require your team to send a follow-up report to each client to share their notes on what they learned about the client's situation and what they identified as priorities. That report could outline the next steps and how they will create value for the client and their team.

Likewise, something as simple as requiring your team to turn in their plan on Friday afternoon for the following week can improve your team's time management, keep them focused on what's important, and multiply their results by using their time wisely. For that matter, sometimes stopping an activity will benefit you, like no longer qualifying the prospective client on the first call. Some might call that heresy, but no activity at all is better than one that creates a negative client experience.

Some of these ideas might find their way into your new vision, but what's more important is to look at your future through a lens that considers which activities will help you do even better in the future. The reason many sales organizations stall is that they rely on "more activity" alone, without recognizing their limitless potential to change what they do.

How will you need to change your team's activities to improve your revenue growth in the coming year?

## Effectiveness Multipliers

As a sales leader, your number-one initiative from year to year should be increasing your sales force's effectiveness, both individually and collectively. Effectiveness multiplies the result of each activity, improving your team's results.

Development is a process, one that takes time. Too many sales organizations believe that training is transformation, but while training can contribute to greater effectiveness, it isn't magic. By theming your year, you can decide what new competencies you need to enable to increase net new revenue. By using a comprehensive cadence, you can use your conversations to glean an understanding of what each individual needs to change to be more effective—as well as the competencies that would benefit your entire team.

There are any number of competencies or character traits that, if enabled or improved, would improve overall growth and possibly boost growth rates. The competency model in Chapter 9 is a good guide for identifying areas where your team would gain from improving their approach. It's important to recognize that improvement often means approaching a familiar activity in a brand-new way.

One straightforward way to improve your results is to recognize the limits of the "why us" approach most salespeople use for a first meeting. As I suggested in Chapter 14, you should protect your sales force from this marketing-created approach, as it provides no value for your prospective clients and often makes them (figuratively) run screaming into your competitor's waiting embrace. It's better to start a conversation with a focus on the client and why they no longer produce the results that once came easy.

Another improvement you might consider is looking at discovery itself as a conversation where the client learns something about themselves, their company, the reason they're struggling to produce the results they need, and their potential to improve. You increase your team's effectiveness by providing them with a way to both learn and teach at the same time. More discovery isn't better than better discovery, especially as measured by the value created for the client.

Tragically, few B2B sales organizations use a framework or methodology for building consensus. Any marginal improvement here will create greater effectiveness in this area, given that ignoring consensus often loses deals and can even kill the client's initiative. For most, building consensus is a new activity, proving again that leading growth requires a behavioral change that improves effectiveness.

These three areas are a worthwhile starting point, but only once you know what will best help your sales team. Take the time to assess your team members, explore your choices, and make a good decision. I would, however, recommend giving yourself three years for a full transformation.

## Asking for Additional Resources

One senior leader I know was so bold as to demand his sales managers double their revenue in the upcoming year, using only their existing resources. No, he wasn't trying to build a pyramid—he just believed that the sales force was doing half of what he expected of them. Because he was new to the company, he had no idea how much time his sales force spent driving to their client sites, a problem he tried to solve by having them make calls to prospects while they were driving to and from client meetings. This ask demoralized his sales managers and salespeople, and I doubt it did their driving any favors either.

Unfortunately, it is not unusual for sales leaders to ask their sales managers to create net new revenue using the same resources. This often indicates that senior leaders are too far removed from the day-to-day experiences of their sales force. When this is true, the leaders can easily underestimate the resources required for consistent growth.

### More Resources in the Field

Imagine you have a territory that is target-rich but you have too few salespeople to pursue the opportunities available to them.

You could do what some sales mangers do and assign each sales-person a larger list of prospects to pursue. While that might seem like a good idea, unless your new list comes with a time machine, your salespeople are not going to be able to capitalize on the opportunities. Asking for more workers is an option, but it also comes with an obligation to increase your quota to help pay the new salary.

Some organizations would benefit from an inside sales func-tion to acquire additional orders from their existing clients, freeing up the field sales force to focus on acquiring clients instead of just acquiring orders. Other organizations may ben-efit from adding a customer success function to ensure they retain clients and avoid the churn that naturally occurs in some industries.

Those who have done the work in this book and improved their results have proven they can be trusted with additional resources, especially if those resources produce additional net new revenue or an increase in their growth rate.

## More Resources for Acquisition and Retention

Your additional resources might also be the additional money you need to acquire new talent or to increase pay for the salespeople who are generating the greatest revenue. You may do this in part as a commission, but there is a strong argument that more direct retention of high performers is necessary, especially when they have many other opportunities available.

Losing a high performer, especially one who continually cre-ated net new revenue, can set you back. One salesperson I know worked for a company where there was a dramatic culture change when a new leader took over. This young leader believed their clients were not going to leave them, as the switching costs were very high, especially as it pertained to their client's production. At some point, the leader decided that he could even withhold the client's data when they moved to a competitor. The salesperson who had won the clients in the first place was upset that his now-lost clients had to sue the company to get their data. He left the company, walked across the street, and took his clients with him. This is an extreme example; this was the company's only salesperson, and when he left they experienced "negative growth."

## More Resources for Sales Enablement

Most sales managers don't ask for the resources they need to develop their team. But if effectiveness is a critical factor when it comes to your growth, you would do well to secure a budget for training and development. You have a role in improving your team's effectiveness, but that role isn't to create methodologies and frameworks and workshops. That work belongs to people who generate and license their content to sales organizations.

Sales technology is another category of resources you may need to acquire to improve your results. I confess that I am not an expert on sales technologies, outside the technology between your two ears. That said, there are tools that will create greater productivity, like databases that contain human-verified phone numbers and email addresses. There are also tools that allow you to record your sales force's phone calls, allowing you to review the recordings, use them for coaching, or show other salespeople what a good sales call sounds like.

Before we move on to planning your next vision, remember that you will need to make changes to your team's activities and improve their effectiveness. You will also likely have to negotiate for more resources to increase your results from year to year.

## How to Use October

As you start to sketch out your vision, you may want to make a list of changes you want to make in the coming year. One way to make this easier amidst the busyness of business is to keep a master document where you collect all of the ideas that you want to consider. Some of these you will actually execute, while others will lay dormant, waiting for the right time. You may want to keep this list of future initiatives on your phone, since it is omnipresent.

This isn't a New Year's resolution, so don't put it off until the last week of December. The ideal time to build your new vision is September, I think, but because Q3 often ends in September, it may be difficult to carve out time to plan and draft. For most sales managers, October is a better time to complete this work because it's the beginning of a new quarter.

The better part of October should be used to prepare for the following year, one that seems to approach even faster during Q4. January is way too late to start worrying about the year that has already started. No matter what quotas your company expects of you, it's your job to create your own goals and targets based on your team's potential. By giving yourself a higher target, you give yourself a buffer, one you may need later.

Before we get into some more technical ideas, we need to back up to July. If you know that you are going to need additional resources, greater headcount, or more money for salespeople, training, or technology, you want to file those requests well before October. Depending on when your year starts and when your leadership settles on a budget, those requests may need to be in several months ahead of time.

## Vision 2.0

Let's go back to the revenue growth formula, the equation we introduced at the beginning of this book:

Existing Revenue – Churn + Net New Revenue = Growth

You are going to need a reasonably good projection of the existing revenue you'll have at the start of next year. One way to calculate this is to look at your team's existing clients and their commitments, so you at least have a good estimate. Next, categorize clients as "safe" when you are certain the client isn't going to defect, and as "at risk" when the client may leave or be stolen away by a competitor. The easiest and saddest part of your calculations is to add up the clients you have already "lost." You want to be conservative, so it may not make sense to remove everything that is "at risk." Instead, look at your past losses due to client churn and use a number you believe is going to be reasonably close.

Now for the hard part, net new revenue. You have to look at which clients each salesperson won to get an idea of what they are likely to do in the future. You should not expect a top-producing salesperson to do less than they did in the past, but you should remove the giant deal that came out of nowhere, as you can't expect such lavish gifts from Fortuna herself each year. No matter their quota, you should likewise not expect a salesperson who is in the bottom quartile to suddenly jump up to the top of the stacked ranking, but neither should you believe they are incapable of increasing their net new revenue by, say, 10 to 15 percent.

## The View Through the Territory and Account Plan

One of the reasons to use a territory and account plan is that by identifying your dream clients, you know which companies you have won, which you haven't won, and which may still be unknown to you and you to them. The point here is to look deeply into each territory to determine where you are going to find your net new revenue and whom it is going to come from.

If you need $10 million in net new revenue in a territory with an estimated $200 million in potential revenue, you need to capture only 5 percent of the total spending in that territory. If you need $10 million in a territory that has only $20 million in spending, you will need a miracle to capture half the revenue in the territory in a single year. You need to know not just how much new revenue to generate, but where you expect your team to get it.

## Focus on What You Really Want

A long time ago, when you read Chapter 1, "Vision," you answered, "What do you want for and from your team?" I gave you my list of ideas, including things like "growth from large clients" and "never needing to answer 'why us' because the salesperson has proven it with the value they create inside the sales conversation."

You will have accomplished some of the things that you put on that initial list during your first year following this program, and those results will help you recognize what comes next for your team. Don't try to boil the ocean in a teakettle. Instead, prioritize your initiatives by the contribution they make to growth. You don't have to do everything all at once. You have a year to make progress, even if some of what you want will take a number of years.

## Leadership Is the Variable to Success

I keep a folder titled "Dumb things smart people say." These quotes all have one thing in common: the belief that two important things are somehow mutually exclusive. You'll have no trouble finding this mutual exclusivity on LinkedIn, especially in the polls that people use to get engagement. So when people ask you to choose, for instance, between helping your clients and making sales, know that the correct answer is "both."

One recent arrival to my folder claimed, "You are not a leader because you are in charge; leadership is about taking care of those in your charge." I have to wonder—if the leader isn't in charge, who the hell is? You already know that you have a responsibility to lead your team, precisely because you are in charge. Otherwise, your company would not have given you a team. You also know you have to take care of your people, helping them grow, improve, and succeed in the workplace and at home.

Leadership is a critical factor in producing results in business—and in any other human endeavor. Leadership is largely concerned with building the future: determining what that future is going to look like, identifying what is necessary to bring it to life, determining a strategy and an action plan, setting a high standard, and developing the people on your team to ensure they achieve their goals and yours.

## The Two Types of Hierarchies

Two kinds of hierarchies exist in nature. The first is called a dominator hierarchy, where the leader is an autocrat and where force is the primary strategy. That's fine for, say, orcs. Among humans, though, force is the choice of the weaker party, one who cannot achieve their goals in a more effective way. You would not enjoy working in a dominator hierarchy (and I wouldn't make it through the first half hour, as I have strong and aggressive responses to bullies, an adaptation to my childhood experience, even though I've since learned to be diplomatic).

The second type of hierarchy is called a growth hierarchy, and the difference should be obvious. As the philosopher Ken Wilber taught me, "atoms to molecules, molecules to cells, cells to organisms." Organisms don't dominate cells, cells don't dominate molecules, and molecules don't harm cells. What is interesting is that when you destroy a molecule, you destroy the cells, but not the atoms. Everything above is gone, but everything below is intact.

A growth hierarchy is one where each member is nurtured and protected, the exact opposite of a dominator hierarchy. You want to lead and build a growth hierarchy.

# Epilogue

ONE REASON I wrote this book is because too many salespeople have been thrust into their roles without any training or development, and without an understanding how to do their number-one job: generate new revenue. Many sales managers were selected for the role because they were highly effective in the role of salesperson, not because they have the natural ability to lead. That might be you, or it might be someone you know. One of the reasons sales managers don't have these strategies and structures is because their sales manager didn't provide them, and neither did that sales manager's manager.

One way to steward the future is by building the next generation of leaders who have experienced what good leadership and good sales management looks and feels like, along with the structure that will improve their ability to succeed. Some of your team members may end up in a sales management role, and one way to judge your effectiveness as a leader is by how many leaders you create—each with their own vision.

I want to thank you for buying *Leading Growth*, reading it, and implementing the strategies, tactics, and structures we've

explored together. I hope you use them to help your team succeed in helping their clients succeed, and to reach their goals
and yours. Nothing in this book is easy to execute, but I believe
it's all worth the effort. I also believe sales management is one of
the more difficult positions one might agree to take on, because
most people don't understand how challenging it is to create net
new revenue—something that only occurs when a salesperson
has a conversation that creates enough value that their prospective client signs a contract and pays for what we sell.

You can reach me at www.thesalesblog.com/leadinggrowth or
on LinkedIn at www.linkedin.com/in/iannarino.

# Acknowledgment

OVER THE COURSE of four books, I have thanked the hundreds of people who have supported me and my work as a writer and author. I am grateful for each of them, but what follows here will be a different type of acknowledgment.

Each of us has certain experiences that provide lessons, some painful, some that leave a mark. Some of these marks are visible to the human eye and others are invisible, but they exist all the same. The internal marks tend to be the ones that cause the most damage. Most of us are softer on the inside than the outside. You know this to be true if you have had the experience of both breaking a bone and having your heart broken by someone you believed loved you. The heartbreak may hurt more than the broken bone.

The nature of our Universe doesn't allow you to reverse time and provide you with a second chance to avoid your mistakes, missteps, and misjudgments. Many people wish for an opportunity to take back certain decisions, believing their lives would be better had they taken a different path.

There is no evidence that the person following a different path would find themselves in a better place. There is, however, evidence that having made a poor decision, the harsh lesson that followed prevented you from repeating it. Nothing prevents one from being burned like touching fire. Most of what you learned came at a price. Having paid dearly for a lesson keeps you from paying for it a second or a third time.

This is an acknowledgment that the way one becomes a good leader is by making mistakes, recognizing them, and making a different decision in the future. It's also an acknowledgment that you are likely to make mistakes in the future, because no leader has a perfect record when it comes to making decisions or leading their team. The best one can do is to lead in such a way that everyone on your team grows while they are part of your team. If you get this much right, two things will be true. First, your team will succeed. But more important, you will have created the legacy of having built the next generation of leaders, most of whom will know how to avoid the mistakes you made.

# About the Author

Anthony Iannarino is a reader, writer, author, speaker, entrepreneur, and a sales leader and trainer. Iannarino has written and published a daily post every day since December 28, 2009, amassing over 4,600 posts on sales, success, leadership, and productivity. The main thrust of his work is human effectiveness. His books have been translated into 18 languages.

# Index